CULTURAL STUDIES

CULTURAL STUDIES

A PRACTICAL INTRODUCTION

MICHAEL RYAN

With Brett Ingram and Hanna Musiol

WILEY-BLACKWELL

A John Wiley & Sons, Ltd., Publication

This edition first published 2010
© 2010 Michael Ryan

Blackwell Publishing was acquired by John Wiley & Sons in February 2007.
Blackwell's publishing program has been merged with Wiley's global Scientific,
Technical, and Medical business to form Wiley-Blackwell.

Registered Office
John Wiley & Sons Ltd, The Atrium, Southern Gate, Chichester, West Sussex,
PO19 8SQ, United Kingdom

Editorial Offices
350 Main Street, Malden, MA 02148-5020, USA
9600 Garsington Road, Oxford, OX4 2DQ, UK
The Atrium, Southern Gate, Chichester, West Sussex, PO19 8SQ, UK

For details of our global editorial offices, for customer services, and for
information about how to apply for permission to reuse the copyright material
in this book please see our website at www.wiley.com/wiley-blackwell.

The right of Michael Ryan to be identified as the author of this work has been
asserted in accordance with the UK Copyright, Designs and Patents Act 1988.

Library of Congress Cataloging-in-Publication Data is available

9781405170505 hbk
9781405170499 pbk

A catalogue record for this book is available from the British Library.

Set in 10.5 on 13 pt Minion by Toppan Best-set Premedia Limited
Printed and bound in Singapore by Ho Printing Singapore Pte Ltd

001   2010

For Mia

Contents

Preface

The word *culture* has always had multiple meanings. In one sense of the word, culture is inseparable from human life. Everything from how we dress to what we eat, from how we speak to what we think, is culture. You only notice this really when you change place and enter another culture. Try crossing a border, any border, and you'll feel it. When I visited Saudi Arabia, I was warned not to speak to women on the street or in other places of potential casual contact. American culture regulates such encounters differently; speech between men and women who are not direct acquaintances is more tolerated so long as inappropriate speech or physical contact is avoided. But clearly, they do things differently and regulate male–female social interactions differently in Saudi Arabia. Culture in this sense is the unstated rules by which we live, rules that regulate our everyday practices and activities without our thinking about them or noticing them.

Culture becomes visible when we travel between "cultures" and when we look back in time to other "cultures" than our own. In Saudi Arabia most men who are part of the extended Saudi families that rule the country wear long loose white robes and red checkered head scarves. The scarves are different one from the other, with each indicating which tribe the man belongs to. Women wear long black robes, some covering their entire faces. One can see them standing looking in shop windows that display colorful Italian women's evening gowns, which can only be worn in Saudi culture in the privacy of one's own home. To do so in public would be an offense to the reigning religious beliefs and practices, the dominant culture. If one travels to the source of those Italian gowns – to Rome, say – one sees a quite different culture that registers itself in a very different style or fashion of dress. Young women wear open blouses that expose decorative brassieres and they look quite different from Saudi women. Italian men also look remarkably different in dress, although similarly uniform in other respects.

At work, many wear what in the West would count as conventional "suits" that consist of formal slacks and jackets with ties. One can see groups of young men outside government office buildings all dressed in the same black suits and looking as uniform as the men one sees in Saudi Arabia.

Culture as a way of life tends to produce a commonality of thought and behavior, as well as conformity with reigning standards, norms, and rules. It is what allows us to live together in communities by giving us shared signs and signals whose meaning we know and recognize. We recognize fellow members of our culture by dress, speech, behavior, and look. In this sense of the word, *culture* means embedded norms all obey usually without thinking about it. The norms are learned as one grows up. One sees others around one adhering to them and imbibes silent lessons from the cultural air one breathes. Within this larger sense of culture, there can be regions and zones, institutional settings with cultures or subcultures of their own. High schools can have quite specific cultures, ranging from the San Fernando Valley to East High in Newark, New Jersey, from a "valley girl" cultural style to a "ghetto" style. Investment banks can have a culture of "cowboy capitalism," in which men compete to make the most risky bets that make the most income. Such cultures change once government increases regulation and imposes greater responsibility. The culture becomes more sober and restrained. The swashbuckling adventuring comes to an end. A more staid, responsible culture takes over.

A more familiar meaning of the word *culture* is the things we humans make when we translate ideas into objects. If the first sense of the word *culture* comprised behaviors and institutions, such things as the norms by which we live, the practices in which we engage (everything from dress to bathing), and the institutions we inhabit and use such as courts, market-places, and workplaces, the second meaning of culture comprises cultural artifacts, such things as the shape we give the built environment (the architecture of buildings, for example), the forms of entertainment we create (such as Hollywood or Bollywood movies), and the music we listen to (be it techno or rap). That list is far from exhaustive of human creativity or of the multiple ways humans create and develop institutions, activities, and things that are fabricated, artificial, and artistic and that count as culture in this second sense of the word.

It is easy to forget that cultural behaviors and institutions may have much to do with cultural artifacts. Whether one is able to write novels depends on whether or not one can afford paper to print it on or whether one has time away from earning a living to engage in the time-consuming

activity of writing. Similarly, in order to make successful musical recordings, one must have not only talent but also a music production company
that has the capital to make your music into marketable recordings.
To engage in the cultural activity of making television shows or movies,
one must work with large economic entities that have the wherewithal to
produce and market your ideas and creations. One might say that culture
in the second sense of artistic objects is only possible if culture in the first
sense as a way of life gives permission. One cannot make good television
shows if there is no television distribution system, for example, and that
presupposes a high level of prosperity of the kind found in such places as
London and Hong Kong but not in the African or South Asian countryside.
Similarly, to write novels, one usually has to be well educated, to know
language well at least and to be trained in how to write. Culture understood
as a norm-guided behavior or as an institution is the house in which culture
understood as an artifact occurs. What this means is that most cultural
products or artifacts embody and express the norms of the culture in which
they are made. But not all.

The culture in which one lives determines the culture that is created
within it, but influence works in the other direction as well. One could even
go so far as to say that the second meaning of culture as human creativity
is our way of modifying the first meaning of culture as civilized normativ-
ity. Creative culture is often accused of being uncivil because it breaks
existing norms and points the way toward the creation of new ones. When
the bohemian movement started in Western Europe in the late nineteenth
century, it was an attempt on the part of creative people to upset the reigning norms of the culture, which were perceived as being too restrictive, too
allied with conservatism, commerce, and a narrow scientific view of knowledge. Women had been instructed throughout the nineteenth century to
be prim and proper and to dress accordingly – tight corsets, body-covering
dresses, and the like. Along came the bohemians in the 1880s who upset
all that. They wore loose clothing that revealed their bodies. Women artists
danced in free style instead of in the prescribed rote forms associated with
"high" culture. Emotional expressiveness replaced formal rigor, and reverie
replaced objective scientific clarity. Drugs, of course, were part of the new
bohemian scene, as was potent alcohol that altered the normal state of
things. Commercial conservative "bourgeois" culture's hold on human
possibilities was shaken, and a new culture eventually was born. We still
live with its legacy today when we dress informally or reveal our bodies
without shame or embarrassment or dance in nonprescribed ways to music

that no one in the nineteenth century would recognize as "legitimate" music. The bohemians were first perceived to be rulebreakers by the keepers of normative culture, but with time, the changes they introduced into cultural life altered for the better the cultural house they and we live in.

To use a contemporary analogy, culture is the software of our lives. It is the program we live by, the rules that determine how we think and act. But it is also the malleable, rewritable script that we ourselves rework and recreate as we live and produce creative works and say and do creative things in our lives. *Culture* is a more inclusive term than *art*, another name for human creativity, because it allows for everyday art and common creativity, something that happens without frames or legitimizing institutions such as galleries or museums or concert halls. When girls take to body piercing and young men to tattooing as a way of "expressing" themselves, of distinguishing their identity from that of others amongst their peers or from their parents' culture, they are being creative culturally in this larger sense. Artists of everyday life, they are practicing an everyday aesthetics that has more to do with lived life than with the frames of institutional art. Indeed, Cultural Studies came into being in Britain in the 1960s and 1970s to a large degree as an examination of such creativity and of the ways it clashed with institutional, legitimate, or formal culture. Punk style, such scholars argued, was significant within the culture precisely because it sought to shatter culture understood as behavior-determining norms. The most interesting tension in culture will occur at the frontier running through everyday life where the normative and the creatively dissonant collide. Normative culture must respect established forms and prescribed practices. It is our way of maintaining the stability of our civil life in communities. Creative culture has less respect for such things; indeed, it is defined as disrespect for whatever would make the new resemble the old. Culture in this sense is human life remaking itself anew every day. It is creative destruction as much as it is system maintenance through embedded normative prescription.

Culture understood as what maintains civility in communities is necessary because nature propels humans toward physical survival in ways that can lead to violence, domination, and injustice. Culture and civility are our ways of tempering those physical urges, but violence, domination, and injustice occur nevertheless, and Cultural Studies has a moral, ethical, and political dimension to the degree that it takes stock of that reality. In some humans, at least, there is a strong drive toward the over-accumulation of social resources, the subordination of others through dominance behavior, deceptive trickery to attain purely expedient and unprincipled ends, and a predatory empiricism that limits knowledge to unimaginative surveying of one's surroundings and of others in order to control for the possibility of danger, with danger consisting of any threat to the over-accumulation of resources and one's position of domination in a hierarchical model of society. As critics of this situation and of this conservative strand of humanity, Cultural Studies scholars tend to be skeptical regarding cultural ideologies that justify domination and over-accumulation. Many are concerned with the cultural forms that result from that human situation, forms that are expressive of the lives of those victimized by it. Some are concerned with the forms of civility, the ways we human have of developing alternatives to violence, domination, and over-accumulation. Others study the way we humans use our creativity to challenge that situation of violence, domination, and injustice or to make artifacts that propel humanity toward new forms of life, new styles, new identities, new ways of being as either individuals or civil communities. It is a rich new field of intellectual endeavor, and this book is designed to introduce you to how it is done and to give you practice in doing it yourself. It is intended to complement *Cultural Studies: An Anthology* (Wiley, 2008), and ideally, you should read the selections in the anthology pertaining to each chapter in this book before plunging into each chapter. That way, you will have the theory or the ideas that I take for granted here at your disposal. I apologize for the fact that the anthology contains no readings to match the chapter entitled "Bodies and Things." That oversight ideally will be corrected in the second edition of the anthology.

Acknowledgments

I am grateful to Elizabeth Bada, Brittany Webb, Diane Garbow, and Jen Giurlano for their help with research for this book.

Alanna Miller was a stellar research assistant and provided a great deal of helpful advice in addition to tons of great library and web material.

My coauthors, Brett Ingram and Hanny Musiol, are to be thanked for their excellent contributions.

1

Policy and Industry

Culture has always been both a physical act as well as an ideational event. It is a combination of talented concept and production mechanism. Talented musical composers in the past depended on wealthy patrons to sustain them while they made music. These days, a talented television artist such as Joss Whedon depends on production and distribution companies such as Fox to have his ideas realized in actuality, and as he discovered when his show *Firefly* was cancelled, commerce is as important as aesthetics in determining the success of one's art.

Because of the profit-driven nature of the culture industries, they aim toward standardization of product to assure continuity of income. Considering the amount of money at stake, any departure from the standard that is financially successful will for the same reason quickly generate copies, and the new quickly becomes standard. Standardization is also necessary because of the nature of the audience, both national and global. That audience is characterized by a range of educational levels and by a related range of aptitudes for understanding audiovisual messages. The term *lowest common denominator* is usually used to describe the way the "mass" culture industries create products that appeal to as wide a selection of people from the highly diverse audiences they address and seek to please. It has become a commonplace to remark that the general audience prefers simple fare with fairly uncomplicated characters, themes, and plot lines. Mass audiences are said to prefer to see their vision of the world endorsed rather than challenged. This has led to a bifurcation in many forms of culture such as film and music. On one side is mainstream art, which is characterized by standard, easily recognized products that appeal to a broad audience and to a lowest common denominator by making significant compromises to suit audience aptitudes. On the other side is marginal art, which usually refers to the independent sector or the avant-garde, where higher levels of formal experiment and thematic innovation are possible because the audience is often small, better educated, and characterized by a more critical worldview at odds with mainstream assumptions.

During the decades after World War II in the US, for example, films from Europe, Asia, and elsewhere were made on low budgets with, often, untrained actors, yet they were very popular with educated audiences because they explored issues that were left out of mainstream Hollywood films of that era. While American films of the 1950s portrayed White suburbia as a world of easily resolved emotional conflicts, where social embarrassment might be the greatest harm that might befall someone, films such as Satyajit Ray's Apu Trilogy portrayed the difficulties of life in situations of poverty. The problems depicted were tangible and material. By the late 1960s and early 1970s, the Hollywood film industry had adapted and begun to make more realistic films such as *Five Easy Pieces* that dealt seriously with human and social problems. The days of the facile plot resolution were gone, apparently forever. The repeal of the Production Code in 1968, a policy that limited the range of subject matter that Hollywood films could cover and the ways controversial subject matter was treated, also made possible a creative opening in mainstream film production. A change in government policy made possible a change in cultural content.

But the US economy sank during the 1970s, the film industry suffered, and to survive it began to make more "blockbuster" films, ones such as *The Godfather* that were guaranteed to earn enormous profits. As a result, US filmmaking changed and once again became more standardized and more mainstream. The least common denominator returned in such film series as *Star Wars* and *Indiana Jones* that contained racial and cultural stereotyping that would have been unacceptable in marginal films made for more educated audiences. As the dominant tone of the country became more conservative in the 1980s, the film industry played to its concerns and made films such as *Top Gun* that celebrated US military power.

But the alternative, marginal, critical, avant-garde audience was still out there, and the film industry rediscovered it in 1989, when a small company named Miramax distributed *sex, lies, and videotape*, a modest film with no stars to carry it in which fairly ordinary people with common moral flaws seek to work out a complex series of relations that involve friendship, betrayal, and adultery. The existing mainstream culture industry could not accommodate such a vision of life. It required a small marginal production company willing to take the risk. The film was bought at the Sundance Film Festival, and along with such films as *Pulp Fiction*, it established mainstream outlets for marginal independent films. New digital film equipment made independent filmmaking cheaper at the same time; more people now had access to filmmaking, and the number of independent productions grew. In response, mainstream companies such as Sony Pictures Classic and Warner Independent began to scour the independent film festival circuit in search of the new zeitgeist. What followed was a long string of small strong films designed for educated audiences that ranged from adaptations of the novelist Henry James to fanciful historical reproductions such as *Shakespeare in Love* to quirky and critical foreign films such as *Il Postino* (*The Postman*). Anarchism, the political flavor of choice amongst the avant-garde, began to assume a place of some importance in films such as *The Matrix* and *V for Vendetta*. If one compares the character of the Joker in the 1989 version of *Batman* with the same character in the 2008 version, one notices a palpable difference between a homey goof-off mainstream audiences might chuckle over and a hardcore anarchist with decidedly non-mainstream ideas about what constitutes fun.

While the culture industry for film might be accused of playing too powerful a determining role, largely shaped by the financial mandate to make a profit at the expense often of intellectual and aesthetic integrity, it also demonstrates, for the same reason, a remarkable ability to expand, change, and absorb the new and the different, even when in theory the new challenges the basic assumptions of the economic system.

If the relation between culture understood as fabricated object and culture understood as a way of life is often economic in character, it is often also a matter of government policy. Many governments seek to counter the power and influence of private economic entities, which play a sizable role in determining what culture is made, by creating "public" television and radio networks. One of the first, the British Broadcasting Corporation, was established in the 1930s self-consciously with the goal in mind of offsetting the influence of "popular" and privately owned, for-profit American radio programming, which was perceived by the British as "lowbrow" or as appealing to tastes that had not been made sophisticated by education. Lowbrow entertainment would be more likely, for example, to be characterized by bodily humor and might lack complex narratives or characters.

The struggle between governments and private economic players continues to the present day. One of the most important recent conflicts concerns the effort by France to protect indigenous cultural production, especially in film and television, from being weakened or destroyed by much stronger private sector cultural producers such as the American film industry. The French decided to protect their domestic audiovisual industries at a time when talks were underway to "liberalize" world trade. Liberalization makes trade between countries as free as possible from government control by removing barriers such as tariffs, quotas, and customs restrictions. Such world trade talks were initially meant to cover all commercial goods. But in 1994, France declared culture to be an exception and argued that cultural goods, because they had a high degree of ideational content and were bound up with the health of the national culture, were not in fact commercial in character. Yes, they were bought and sold, but their cultural value in maintaining a distinct French cultural way of life had also to be taken into account. They helped to define French culture. If all French cultural production disappeared because it could not match the market power of American cultural products, harm would be done to the idea and the reality of a distinct French cultural identity. There would be no more French film or distinctly French literature. The argument assumed that one culture, because of language, history, and a common way of life, is different from another and has a distinct identity apart from others. The French argued that American mass cultural products such as Steven Spielberg's film *Jurassic Park* create an international "monoculture," much as McDonald's, when spread all over the world, runs the risk of fostering international culinary uniformity. In monoculture, culture everywhere would be the same. There would be no Chinese movies, no Australian movies, and no African movies. Only Hollywood would thrive because it is the most efficient, skilled, and popular film production source. According to David Ricardo, whose theories of international economic liberalization guide the effort to make the world marketplace entirely free of government supervision, some countries do some things better than others. If American makes better movies, then others should buy films from America and ship to America the things that they make best, such as French wine and cheese. France should stop trying to make films if they cannot compete on the world market. Let American make the movies since they do that more efficiently, and let France stick to what it does best – cooking, wine, and tourism.

The pure theory of economic liberalization clearly ignores the question of cultural identity and marginalizes the issue of cultural survival. The French made their case by noting that, were the market allowed to determine what audiovisual cultural products the French consumed, French products would not fare well, and French cultural production would wane, especially in film and television. American films account for 85 percent of world box office revenue, while European films account for just 5 percent of the US market. In 1998, of the top 100 grossing films worldwide, 88 were American and 7 of the remaining 12 were co-produced in the US. With a few British exceptions, all of the films on the list of top 100 grossing films of all time are American. American film producers clearly have a knack for making popular films that have worldwide appeal. A study of how they are made shows why this is the case. American filmmakers have mastered the art of efficient narrative; very little time in US films is devoted to dialog that is not connected to the evolution of the storyline. In contrast, French films are renowned for being "talky," for including dialog on philosophical and personal issues that is not efficiently connected to the narrative. Moreover, American films have "high" production values that depend on strong funding not available to filmmakers in other parts of the globe. A *Jurassic Park* costs huge amounts of money to make, money that is not available in other nations. The average cost of making a film in the US in 2007 was nearly $80 million, compared to $7.4 million in France.

The French government instituted policies based on the idea of "cultural exception" in 1994. And the European Community (EC) government followed suit. In France currently US film producers are limited to 60 percent of the market. While the EC requires that all television channels carry at least 50 percent European programming, France has increased that amount to 60 percent, with 40 percent devoted to national French programming. This allows such "talky" shows as *Apostrophe*, a popular book discussion program, to thrive. At the same time, France taxes movie ticket receipts and uses the funds to subsidize domestic filmmaking, something American critics say should not be allowed because the US government does not do the same thing for its filmmakers. French filmmakers are given loans that have to be repaid only when the films they make turn a profit. The results of these quotas and subsidies are striking. The French share of the French film market in 1996 was 35.4 percent. In other countries where similar protections for domestic filmmaking are not in place, the share is uniformly lower. In Spain, American films in 2002 accounted for 70 percent of the market while Spanish films only had 12 percent. The protections put in place in 1994 in France clearly had an effect. In 1995, the US share of the French market fell to 54.2 percent from 60.5 percent. In Europe in general, where similar protections of domestic film industries have been put in place, the share of the market rose to 28.8 percent for European films in 2007 from 25 percent in 2005. Compared to the 85 percent market share it holds worldwide, the US attained just 59.1 percent of the market in 2007 in Europe. So protection does seem to nurture domestic film production.

Critics of the policy of cultural exception argue that protection will eventually weaken French film production. By not competing, French filmmakers lose the impetus and means to make their products better. This, the argument goes, accounts for why only one in five French films gets exported to the US and why, of the top 25 films by box office gross in Europe in 2007, only one film – *La Mome*, which never made it to the US – was French (nineteenth place). Protection, the argument goes, also decreases an industry's chances of competing successfully in the world market. Europeans are nowhere near attaining the 85 percent global market share US films routinely secure.

But it is worth noting, nevertheless, that European film production is gaining in strength rather than weakening as a result of these policies. In 2005, Europeans made 789 films, up from 761 in 2004. During the same period, American film production fell from 593 to 453 films. The average annual increase in public funding for audiovisual production in Europe during this period was 10 percent. So there seems to be no correlation between government subsidies and a weakening or loss of industrial vitality, as the critics of the policy suggest. Moreover, the anti-exception argument fails to take culture into account as a reason for why Americans do not watch or want to watch French films. French film culture is less committed to mass audience conventions that make films popular in America, and American culture, which is deficient in the way it sensitizes students to foreign cultures, may account for why Americans find European films in general to be too alien and too difficult to comprehend. They are not "entertainment."

Nevertheless, the fact that so few French films are as popular with French viewers as US films suggests that the greater funding available to American filmmakers does pay off at the box office. The continued, unbroken skill development that is the legacy of the US's industrial history in film production (no wars shattered the US industry and skill development continued through World War II, drawing on expatriate Europeans such as Fritz Lang, Jean Renoir, and Alfred Hitchcock) gives American films an edge even with "loyal" French viewers. The differences in popularity are not extreme, however. French films such as *Taxi 4* and *Ensemble, c'est tout* (*Together, It's Everything*) earned only slightly less ($5.3 and $3.3 million gross, respectively) than American films such as the twenty-fifth-place film *Ghost Rider* ($5.3 million box office gross) in 2007. One must bear in mind as well that France only has 63.4 million people, compared to 305 million in the US. And the US has nearly 40,000 screens compared to 30,000 for all of Europe. The American industry can therefore count on high levels of domestic income that allow expensive and internationally appealing products to be made. Nevertheless, France's national market share in 2006 was an impressive 44.6 percent, and seven of the top 10 films were French.

National market share for one's own films does not make up for an absence of a share of international markets. European films attained a 4.9 percent market share in the US in 2007, but only 11 percent of those films were French. French film culture would appear to be talking to itself, not to others. This would seem to bear out the argument that France's film subsidies foster national cultural insularity. Anti-exceptionalists argue that they require a knowledge of French culture and history to be appreciated and are seen by an increasingly specialized audience. A single national style is inimical, the argument goes, to real cultural diversity.

But diversity of another kind is an additional benefit of the French and European policies. Films from "third" countries in Africa, Latin America, and Asia are provided a space in the European market that they would not otherwise have if market forces alone were determinant. As a result, from 2002 to 2006, 1,324 new films from third countries were distributed in Europe, accounting for 18.5 percent of all the new titles. This opening in the market has coincided with an increase in film production in third countries. European policies that restrict American market power are thus helping to nurture filmmaking in areas of the world that lack the financial clout the US industry possesses. The proportion of new films in Europe that came from third countries increased from 14.7 percent in 2002 to 21.4 percent in 2006. During the same period, few if any African films were distributed in the US, a loss in terms of broadening the awareness of Americans regarding other parts of the globe that is not easy to tally numerically in the way that a gain or loss in market share is.

In addition, the argument for liberalization in the relation between government and the culture industries assumes that one country's products are better than another's if they succeed in reaching a wider audience and earning more money. This purely economic argument leaves out two considerations.

The first is the standard we use to determine quality. American films are popular worldwide because US filmmakers have mastered particular forms of filmmaking that are based in predictable, easily recognized conventions. Everyone around the world knows what to expect when they go to an installment of *Mission Impossible* or *Pirates of the Caribbean*. These forms are simple and uniform from one film to the next; they resemble the forms that one finds in cultural stories from around the world, stories of heroes and of combat or of love and intrigue between rivals. They lack complexity and are insular in their own way. They may not be nationally or culturally insular, but they focus audience attention on a very limited set of concerns from life. They do not explore beyond the boundaries of the generic forms. To an extent, then, they promote a greater insularity of vision than French films that deal with specifically French topics and that require, to be understood, some knowledge of French culture. Such films generally seek to expand the perspective with which people view the world and understand life.

The second consideration is the need to preserve cultural diversity worldwide. European policies that protect domestic culture industries foster diversity by protecting cultural forms that would die out if they were obliged to compete on equal terms with far more financially powerful players such as the US film industry. Without such protections, a few might survive who could imitate the US model of success by making films with simple narratives, highly conventional characters, and uncontroversial themes. But many others who favor complex narratives, unconventional characters, and critical themes would not thrive, and what would result would be a great deal of uniformity in global culture.

Ultimately, the debate comes down to a question of value. Which do we value more – an economic model that places the ideal of perfect freedom for powerful players, who could dominate and monopolize all markets, over all other considerations, be they aesthetic or cultural, or the ideal of preserving different cultural traditions for that end alone without any economic justification being necessary. If indeed we succeeded in creating a global monoculture in which only US films were seen because they were the most successful at reaching a common global audience, would that be a good thing? Would it be justified by the fact that money was being efficiently made by American owners of the US film industry? As with so many things, it is a matter of choice.

Student Exercise

Governments often institute policies designed to guarantee what is called the public interest. A public interest is one that serves the good of the whole community rather than the good of one particular group or private interest. The French government chose to serve such an interest when it decided to limit the market share of American films in France and to make it possible for French culture industries to survive and help preserve France's distinct cultural identity.

This decision was based on the recognition that the unregulated economic market favors those with financial power. By definition, their interests are private rather than public; the purpose of their activities is to make wealth for themselves, not to do good for the entire community.

While private economic actors portray themselves as purely private and not at all dependent on government support or assistance that obligates them to serve the public good or community interest, the media that distribute radio, television, new media, and film to us often consist of a mix of public and private mechanisms. While cable lines are private, they must come to your home over telephone lines on public land donated for that purpose, and while radio and television stations are themselves private in most instances, the broadcast band or what used to be called the *airwaves* is owned by the public and supervised by the government, which distributes it to private business owners.

The limited number of broadcast bands, some would argue, places an obligation on private owners or users of those bands to be sure to serve the public good in their programming because not all points of view will be represented by the limited number of owners of the airwaves. This argument gave rise to something called the *Fairness Doctrine*.

Determine what the Fairness Doctrine was, and write a brief summary of its meaning and its history.

What purpose was it meant to serve, and why did the US government feel that the doctrine was required?

Try to determine if the doctrine actually did influence the content of programming or did achieve the ends it was designed to serve.

The doctrine was eliminated in 1987 by conservatives who argued that the doctrine restricted free speech. They claimed broadcasters were afraid to air controversial material for fear of losing their license. Do you think the doctrine fostered or restricted the discussion of controversial material? Can you find any evidence to support your position?

Consider the following evidence that the absence of regulation (such as the Fairness Doctrine) on controversial issues actually leads to a limiting of viewpoints. Of 432 stations that had sold advertising time to one side of a ballot issue while the doctrine was still in force, 31 percent initially refused to accept that they had an obligation to present an opposed view; 44 percent of that group still refused to broadcast the opposed viewpoint once informed of their obligation. In other words, without an authority to make them represent all sides of a controversy, the side without the wherewithal to buy airtime would be underrepresented. The absence of the doctrine would in fact chill free speech because it allowed money, not ideas, to determine the outcome of public debate. Not all broadcasters were reluctant to air opposing viewpoints to those willing to pay. All of those who did accept the obligation of the fairness doctrine, on the other hand, did air opposing positions. Non-enforcement, in combination with changing market conditions fostered by deregulation, would seem to limit controversy.

Has the elimination of the doctrine made any difference?

Has access to the media by small, less powerful, or marginalized groups or voices decreased? The conservative side of the political spectrum is quite powerful in America, and it accounts for a major portion of the owners of the large media outlets such as Fox News, whose Rupert Murdoch is a famous conservative. Have right-wing voices in the mass media increased as a result of the elimination of the doctrine? And has access by left-wing points of view decreased – at least in the mainstream mass media such as television network news? In 1990, there were just 100 conservative talk radio shows; by 2003, there were 1,350. Did the elimination of the Fairness Doctrine play a role, do you think, in this development?

Is television news any different now than it was, say, 40 or 50 years ago when the doctrine was in force? The doctrine prevented the news from being used for purely partisan purposes. Is that still the case?

A major argument against the continuation of the doctrine was that new media such as the Internet multiply the number of outlets for diverging points of view and different political opinions. There is no longer scarcity of the kind that made the doctrine originally necessary. Do you agree? Does the multiplicity of Internet outlets balance the power of, say, a Fox News or a CNN? Should such powerful media entities still be required to address a "public interest"? Would that constitute a restriction of their rights of free speech? Or should the loudest and most powerful media still be held accountable?

Sources

On the evolution of Hollywood, see Michael Ryan and Douglas Kellner, *Camera Politica: Politics and Ideology in Contemporary Hollywood Film* (Bloomington, Ind., 1988). For a discussion of the French policy of "cultural exception," see Kim Eling, *The Politics of Cultural Policy in France* (Basingstoke, UK: 1999), Tyler Cower, "French Kiss-Off: How Protectionism Has Hurt French Films," *Reason Magazine*, July 2008, http://www.reason.com/news/show/30691.html; Alan Riding, "Filmmakers Seek Protection from US Dominance," *New York Times*, February 5, 2003, http://www.globalpolicy.org/globaliz/cultural/2003/0205film.htm; and David Wachtel, *Cultural Policy and Socialist France* (New York, 1987). On the Fairness Doctrine, see Pat Aufderheide, "After the Fairness Doctrine: Controversial Broadcast Programming and the Public Interest," *Journal of Communication* 40, no. 3 (September 1990): 47–72.

2

Place, Space, and Geography

Culture is inseparable from location. Early human communities organized themselves differently under the influence of different locations and environments. Such ambient influences as climate, soil quality, and availability of building materials contributed to what kinds of cultures were possible or likely to develop. In turn, culture created and left its mark on its spatial location, transforming the landscape in meaningful ways that embodied the values, ideas, and needs of the particular community. Some developed migratory communities in response to an environmental scarcity of resources. Settlements were temporary rather than permanent; institutions such as courts did not assume physical shape in buildings devoted exclusively to the task of the adjudication of conflicts. Other communities, relying on a greater availability of resources, were able to create urban centers and lead more settled lives. If migratory communities maintained civility through tribalism, patriarchy, and custom, such urban communities organized themselves around institutions such as laws and courts, markets and government buildings, and community baths and military barracks. Each kind of local physical world made possible a different kind of cultural world, and in response, humans recreated a new physical landscape, turning mud to brick, brick to buildings, and buildings to institutions with meaning in that particular community. If you visit Rome today, you will see stones lying about the old Forum that seem to have no meaning, but put them back in place in your imagination, and you see vibrant, living institutions that sustained the legal, political, and religious culture of the ancient city. What Cultural Geography teaches us is that if the world around us shapes our lives, we also make the world around us over in ways that embody and embed our thoughts, imaginings, ideals, and meanings. We turn stones into meaningful emblems of our civil agreements and shared values. Cultural Geography is concerned with the way we humans put meaning, politics, and ideas into physical shape when we remake the physical world.

The interplay between human culture and physical environment is always two-way. What kind of community develops in response to an environment affects the kinds of cultural practices the community engages in, and those practices in turn shape and reshape the physical environment, turning it into a human-made landscape. Migratory communities usually did not possess writing or a transmittable culture of learning. Such things were not needed for the society to function. The spoken word was paramount, and the wisdom and the values that bound the community together were often transmitted from one generation to the next through chanted or spoken songs or tales such as Homer's *Iliad*, stories of martial courage that taught young men and women the ideals that the community felt were necessary for its survival. The culture of China was more highly organized. Because of high levels of agricultural production, the Chinese were able to develop institutions such as schools, courts, and governments. This much more institutional culture was transmitted through writing. The religion promoted by the government emphasized values such as respect for authority and self-restraint, rather than the Greek martial virtues, which would have been at odds with Chinese culture's bent toward a highly organized, even bureaucratic kind of social existence.

Culture is spatial in several ways. Populations are distributed geographically with cultural differences manifesting themselves most palpably as differences of place (between, say, the culture of China and the culture of the United States, two geographic regions). Culture is also information that is transmitted spatially. It diffuses over terrain, bringing the landscape within the reach of the ideas and conventions of that particular culture. Settlers brought a new religious ideology to North America in the seventeenth century that eventually replaced the indigenous religious ideology. Culture is spatial also in that it enables power relations that involve the imposition of one spatial region's will on another region, as when regional languages in France such as Bretonne and Occitan were subordinated and subsumed to the language of the Franks, which became the "national language" known today as "French." Culture understood as a way of life particular to a community is also spatial, of course, in that such "ways" vary according to location. The way of life of urban Caribbeans in London or New York is different from that of rural Indians in terms of dress, music, access to new cultural technologies, and so on. If one factors in economic differences, spatial differentiations in ways of life can appear within the same location. Someone living on the Upper East Side of Manhattan in a luxury high-rise apartment will have different cultural experience from someone living homeless on the streets below.

Culture is also spatial in that it provides us with a mapping mechanism that allows us to move through space as we live. It provides a means to assign meaning to events and things in the world so that we can negotiate our way through life, knowing what stop signs mean, for example, or particular kinds of gesture, dress, and words. Such means of interpretation also vary geographically, as when the same cultural artifact (a movie like *Rambo*, for example) means quite differently in different locations because different cultural grids or schemas of interpretation are applied to it. In a western interpretive context, the movie might mean "heroic western male successfully exercises violence against Asian nemeses," while in an Asian interpretive context such as Tonga, it means "heroic fighter against oppressors," with "Asian" disappearing as a significant meaning. In this sense, culture is always perspective, the place from which we view the world, and that place will always be spatially limited and geographically circumscribed. It embodies our gender, our personality, our community, and our race to the degree that those manifest themselves as languages for knowing the world. To know as a White Western European living in the US as I do is to see the world from one location, not another, to give expression to the schemes of one culture and not another. Culture, then, is always situated, always located, always spatial, and always geographic. It is the expression of where we are. Finally, culture is geographic and spatial in an economic sense. When International Monetary Fund loans to countries like Jamaica mandate that local onion farmers must accept competition from low-cost corporate producers like Dole, the spatial and cultural world is transformed. Small farms disappear as income disappears, and the culture of entire Jamaican valleys is erased because there is no longer a market for their products.

Culture transforms the physical world. It is the tool with which we impose civility on a natural world that is inherently uncivil, violent, and meaningless. Landscape can thus be said to be a distillate of culture. Every time we modify a natural landscape by building on it or reshaping it, we invest it with our intentions, our ideas, and our meanings. A landscape comes to have meaning when it ceases to be a simple physical object and is invested with our needs, designs, and imperatives. It becomes like a sign, something that can be read as having an idea behind it, much as a stop sign, while being a red metal physical object, also contains embedded within it the idea "Under penalty of law, you must cease movement here." It comes to embody concepts and institutions that are not tangible and physical but that are present in it nevertheless. To understand it, to "read" its meaning, we have to decipher it, translating what is physically there into the idea it embodies or the cultural concepts it contains. This activity is much like reading a book, which consists of physical objects – black marks on a page – which we in the process of reading translate into ideas. Those ideas in turn are signs that can be interpreted or deciphered because they usually refer to cultural concepts that lie behind them, making them important to us and giving them meaning for us. You turn the marks on this page into ideas because I have informed them with design and intention, with ideas from my mind, but those ideas come from an intellectual culture active in schools and universities in which I participate and in which you are now participating. Having joined that culture, you can absorb its ideas by reading these signs.

Every time you move through a built human environment, a transformed physical landscape, you are moving through something like a book or text, a collection of signs whose meaning derives from the intentions of those who made the environment what it is and the cultural ideals and ideas that lie behind those intentions. Simply by living in that environment, one learns and absorbs those meanings. One shapes ones life in accordance with the imperatives the landscapes contain – as when one goes shopping at a mall instead of in an urban downtown area. One gives assent thereby to a particular modernizing economic project imposed on the community by a particular economic group – the commercial or business class who decided malls were more profitable than downtowns. And one learns to behave in accordance with the dictates for behavior they have successfully inscribed in the landscape. While landscapes are places where one finds meaning, then, they are also economic events and sites where the relations of power in a society manifest themselves palpably.

Some of the meanings landscapes contain are historical; some are social and economic, some a matter of ideology or philosophy, and some are political; but they are all cultural in the sense that they are artifacts we have made with our minds. As a result, they are part of our way of life. They are objects of our creation that serve our needs as members of a particular human community. But "we," of course, are not singular. We as human communities are divided by gender, race, income, and belief. Cultured landscapes embody those divisions. Greek houses were organized around inner realms, hidden from the public street world, where women were confined. The physical world embodied a political power relation between the genders. The difference between downtown Philadelphia, where wealthy whites live, and uptown north Philadelphia, where poor blacks live, is remarkable; it is the difference between the glitz and glamour of commerce and the blight of closed stores, between neat clean streets and littered broken ones. The cultural difference is a physical, economic, and racial difference.

Cultural history can be read through landscapes. One sees there a record of past decisions that express values. The American superhighway system is a record of a choice made in the 1950s, when conservatives from the business community were in power, to privilege profitable car production over more useful but much less profitable public transportation, which in subsequent decades was dismantled after having thrived for decades before the 1950s. America, as a result, became a culture of cars rather than a culture that expressed and addressed a community need (as in Europe where socialists assured that public transportation would survive and thrive). Differences in landscape indicate differences in cultures or changes within the same culture. As the US became more urban and industrial, the farmland around cities was eaten up by suburban housing developments first, then later by large industrial "parks." If one walks through areas of American cities that are in the process of being gentrified, that is, refurbished in order to attract wealthy renters or buyers, one sees residues of an older culture embodied in the architectural details of the buildings. Those details are often ornate and purely decorative rather than functional; they pertain to a cultural moment when wealthy people could afford to decorate houses. The gentrified equivalents lack all such decoration. Theirs is a culture that is more given to cleanness of line and an ideal of the efficient and profitable use of materials – much like the new culture of wealth that makes the gentrification possible. It too thrives on reducing costs (often wages and the value from enterprise assigned to labor instead of the investor class or the business management class), and that reduction appears in the physical buildings in the form of sheets of cheap metal that perform functions that in the past would have been performed by now expensive brick construction.

Human labor on landscapes takes place over time, and as a result, it is always layered. One generation's meanings will usually be constructed on top of those of previous generations. Built landscapes often consist of several levels, each with its distinct historical feel or meaning. In urban landscapes, very different kinds of buildings, for example, can exist side by side, with each often embodying very distinct historical meanings.

They refer to realities or cultural concepts from different times and different kinds of human activity on the landscape. If you walk out the back entrance of Back Bay Station in Boston, Massachusetts, for example, you will see on one side red brick buildings from the nineteenth century that once were single-family homes for the newly wealthy who crowded into this area – a bay that was filled in to create solid land for new houses – during an economic boom. On many of the houses, you see Christian crosses, emblems of the religious ideology that provided the occupants with a sense of virtue and value in their lives. Now the houses for the most part are multifamily dwellings, split up into three apartments to accommodate a new population of urban professionals, many of them young, and many without children. The houses have been transformed from large family homes to suit a different need and serve a different function; their meaning as physical objects has changed as a result.

On the other side of the railway station you will see examples of two more recent architectural styles, one called *modern*, and the other *postmodern*. The modern style was dominant in the middle of the twentieth century till its end, and it is associated with the tremendous growth of US capitalism after World War II. It is a style you have probably all encountered in your lives – straight tall glass buildings that have little ornamentation or adornment and seem designed simply to serve a particular function. Most are "office buildings," in that they house economic organizations such as banks and corporations whose workers have offices in the building. If the red brick homes embody a cultural ideal of family-based capitalism, in which the wealth generated by the economy is used to make homes informed by Christian values whose purpose is to instill virtues in children that sustain that particular model of social organization, the office buildings represent a culture in which work has become more organized and routinized, to the detriment of the ideal of individual moral development. Most of the corporations in the tall buildings could not care less if their workers are Christian or Hindu, Buddhist or Jain. The modernist paradigm emphasizes rationality over religion. Architecture is no different. Function is what matters, the work that functional people do to supply value to the economic organization. The organization takes precedence to all other considerations and ideals. Its sharp straight lines and efficient looking design speak to this imperative.

The building directly in front of you is called *postmodern* because it is not simple and functional; straight lines have been replaced by multiple diverse architectural elements and motifs that seem borrowed from several styles, including that of the red brick houses to your right. It looks like a model of a red brick house that has been built onto a modern building that has been modified to look almost classical, with hints of columns. There are decorative motifs like those in the older red brick buildings, but there is none of the sense of meaning. Postmodern architecture links to the past without embracing its values. Christian symbols were obviously taken quite seriously by the builders of the red brick buildings; these decorative elements seem present in the postmodern building just for the fun of it. There is no sense, as in the red brick buildings, of rootedness in a culture of religious moral values. The cultural world the building embodies might be one in which everything is a little bit up in the air, like the building itself, which lacks a single coherent style or dominant ideal. Everything about it seems a little haphazard or contingent (there by chance rather than necessity), even though roughly in harmony. But that might be a good embodiment of our contemporary postmodern culture, one in which old values no longer hold and in which a variety of discourses – religious, political, economic, and social – contend for our attention and our allegiance. No single story – as in the Christian cultural world of the red brick buildings – accounts for every dimension of our lives in a unified way guided by a single big narrative (the story of Christian suffering and redemption). Things are more up in the air these days, debatable, contingent, or unsettled and easily changed. There are many small narratives instead of just one big one to explain our lives to us. Of this building, you will either think, "What a mess" or "How interesting," depending on your taste. Critics of modern life see this style as embodying the de-centered character of contemporary existence. Gone are the old verities that held nineteenth-century society together around a common set of values. We no longer strive to be moral people in a small social context overseen by a church community and defined by others' opinions of our actions. Our identities are more fluid and multiple, less localized in one single cultural model. Our identities are no longer linked to clear, bounded ethnic cultural traditions. We engage in many cultural traditions. We no longer only marry solely within our own ethnic group or raise our children in one ethnic cultural tradition. "America" is internally transnational these days, a hodgepodge of different, mixed makeups that cannot be called an identity. We are, many would say, more postmodern, and the building in front of you is an expression of that new cultural reality.

The way these buildings embody American culture becomes more evident if you think of why Al Qaeda felt justified in attacking the US by attacking two of its of its most famous buildings – the towers of the World Trade Center in New York City. The straight modernist lines of those buildings and the way they projected in their verticality a sense of economic power were signs for the attackers of the US imperial reach into their countries and cultures by its support for Israel instead of Palestine, by its overthrowing of democratic governments in places like Iran to install pro-US dictatorships that made oil more accessible, and by its stationing of armies in Arab countries in a way reminiscent of the Crusades, when the West invaded the Holy Land. In Cultural Geography, much of what is studied is tangled up with the West's imperialist past. What languages are spoken in a geographic region, what laws and institutions exist, and even people's relationship with their environment is related to who had power in the past and who has power now. Physical symbols like the World Trade Center towers are tied to issues of transnational power. If to Americans the towers connoted beauty, grace, and human achievement, to the attackers they signified something much more pernicious. They were less a symbol of exalted ideals than they were a metonym, a figure or sign that was connected to other realities that meant pain, disgrace, and humiliation to Arabs and Muslims. It may seem odd to call the terrorist attack of 9/11 the expression of a clash of cultural meanings, but considered in the frame of Cultural Geography, that is what it was.

If quite disparate meanings can converge in built objects, the meaning of landscape can also be changed dramatically and intentionally. Some areas are objects of veneration because they pertain to certain religious traditions. They cease to be a simple piece of rock. The Yellowstone River Valley was such a place for the local indigenous people up until the nineteenth century, but once that natural site was taken over by Americans, it changed meaning, became a "national park," and evolved into a tourist attraction that is sought not for its religious value but for its use as a distraction from work life. The geographic change changed the economy of the surrounding region as well.

Something similar happened in Mystic, Connecticut, in the US during the decades of the 1990s and 2000s. The site at the mouth of a river was originally a settlement of the local indigenous people, a group that the European settlers who came in the seventeenth century called Pequots. The Pequot settlement was eliminated in a massacre of the tribe in 1637. That site today is a housing development, and until recently, a statue of the man who led the massacre, John Mason, stood there. It was removed to a museum after the Pequots began to revive and acquire economic resources through gambling enterprises. Mystic's meaning changed from "site of white settler military triumph that should be celebrated and memorialized" to "site of a morally dubious event that harmed a local population whose feelings should be taken into account – even if belatedly."

What constitutes "Mystic" has also changed with time. Originally, it was a post road settlement at the top of the river, about two miles from the mouth of the river where the current "Mystic" stands. But it was easier to cross the river closer to the river mouth, at Mystic Crossing. So eventually that spot became Mystic, and the former Mystic became Old Mystic. Later, in the 1960s, a developer built a false village filled with shops near the new superhighway called *Olde Mysticke Village*. And for many years that was "Mystic" to many tourists, who did not realize there was a real town a mile away on which this false one was based. It was not in the developer's interest to tell them. Similarly, Old Salem, in North Carolina, constructed an old-seeming village for tourists with all of the physical objects of the old village but removed from the context of the actual village.

Mystic thrived economically in the nineteenth century, and one of the most noticeable remaining elements of that built environment are the "captains' houses" that line the river. They belonged to successful merchant and whaling ship captains who were part of the triangular trade between the West Indies, Europe, and the US across the Atlantic. Proximity to water paid off, and the houses reflect a high degree of wealth in their use of land and in such stylistic elements as non-functional, neoclassical columns. Most, however, while ostentatious in size, embody the virtue of simplicity that this Protestant culture favored over more ornate and decorative styles. Further away from the river, one can see houses built later in the nineteenth century that are more decorative and that include such things as Queen Anne's lace moldings on the porches and under the eaves. By the turn of the twentieth century, the older Protestant culture was waning, and people became less retrained in their expression of their wealth. It became less of a moral fault to be ostentatious or interested in beauty for beauty's sake.

It is difficult now to imagine that Mystic was ever poor, but halfway through the twentieth century, the captains' houses fell into disrepair. The sea-based economy had become a memory, and the mills that took its place lapsed when it became cheaper to do the work elsewhere. Working people took the place of the captains in the large old houses that were now rented. All of that began to change in the 1950s, when the national highway system was built. Some local merchants arranged for the highway to curve down toward Mystic so that one could see the town from the road. This costly diversion allowed the town to revive, helped by a "seaport" museum that collected together pieces of the past, moving buildings from various places to create a new artificial town on the site of one of the old ship-building yards that used to line the river in the nineteenth century. The museum succeeded by creating a sense of a simulated town in which certain features of nineteenth-century life were on living display, from a blacksmith forge to a newspaper and an apothecary. While these elements of life were juxtaposed incongruously, they nevertheless conveyed the sense of a diverse culture and economy. They were not a realistic representation of actual life in Mystic, but that was not the point. They served as a plausible simulation of that life. Even if the artificial town was not historically accurate, it managed to create certain meanings for visitors that allowed them to conceive and imagine life in nineteenth-century Mystic.

The changes in the landscape of Mystic were not over. While the museum drew crowds, few people visited the actual downtown. A few tourist shops existed, but for the most part, the town had a local feel. There was a "notions" store that sold knitting and sewing supplies and a shoe repair shop. There was one upscale clothing store and a few others that catered to the middle class. A diner sold inexpensive meals and had a 1950s aura about it. There were no upscale restaurants, and the one hotel was fairly dingy and old-fashioned. The beauty of the river mouth did draw those with money, and someone had built condominiums along the river to accommodate them. But the town had a functional local feel to it while also being a part-time, summer tourist attraction.

Then, a recession came in 1989, and the local economy suffered. Newly arrived younger merchants realized something had to be done to increase their income. So they organized a movement with state funding to turn Mystic into *Mystic Coast and Country*, a tourist destination that would be advertised across the country. Two local indigenous tribes had built casinos in the meantime, and they were drawing customers that, the merchants decided, could be lured down to Mystic. As a result of the campaign, the culture of Mystic changed. Tourism became a year-round business; crowds, which used to be limited to the summer, became a permanent feature of life in the narrow main street. The notions shop closed and was replaced by an expensive rug store, then an upscale toy store. The shoe repair shop disappeared and was replaced by a shop that sold interesting expensive clothes. More upscale clothes shops appeared, and a fine Italian restaurant opened in the newly renovated hotel. The local lumber yard, housed in an old nineteenth-century building along the river (on land that had suddenly become quite valuable), closed and was torn down and replaced by an open grassy area, where the local Chamber of Commerce decided that tourists could stroll and take a break from shopping. Locals who now needed knitting supplies or shoes repaired had to drive to the mall or the next town over.

A culture can clearly take many forms in the same place or location. And even in one location, there can be multiple cultures. These cultures influence each other and the world around them. To the East of Mystic is a spit of land called Stonington Borough on which sit, all crowded together, a hundred or so old homes, some quite beautiful, all the products of the sea economy's wealth. For years, this place was home to Portuguese fishermen who were left over from the old seagoing economy. Their quite religious culture is still palpable in the small fishermen's religious society building and in the annual Blessing of the Fleet, a Roman Catholic ceremony. Go down to the wharves where the fishing boats come and go and you'll see men who look like they just came from Lisbon, Portugal. But with time and the increase in car travel, the Borough has become home to more and more weekenders from New York City. This cultural diffusion is exhibited through the geography. Gone are the grocery stories and meat shops that sustained local inhabitants early in the twentieth century, and on the weekend during the winter, the place seems deserted except for the permanent small population of wealthy homeowners who sustain the several restaurants. The culture of the Borough has changed with time, moving, like Mystic, from a local network of lived relations to a connectedness with very distant lives and places. People no longer know each other on the basis of neighborhood or shared local school experience; instead, they may use the same investment banker or frequent the same antique shop or dine regularly at the same restaurant or go sailing at the same time from the local yacht club. The old school building was in any event long ago converted to condominiums, although you can still meet men on the docks who recall attending the school and seeing their fathers from the windows during class returning from fishing trips. If you go to a certain restaurant/bar in the Borough of a weeknight, you will encounter a mildly alcoholic culture. People stay seated all evening, imbibing drink after drink, talking to each other. At the tables sit families of wealthy weekenders from New York or wealthy locals enjoying a meal out together.

Nearby, the city of New London, where some of the patrons of the bar own rental properties, is distinguished culturally from the Borough in many ways. Because many Whites left, the city is largely inhabited by ethnic minorities who do service labor at hotels or the local Native American casinos. They live in apartments cut out from old buildings that used to be summer homes for wealthy people from elsewhere back when New London was a resort destination in the late nineteenth century. Most do not possess cars, and they take buses out into the countryside where the casinos are located. One of them, a Hispanic woman who is a single mother of three children, works the night shift while her children are sleeping. There is no sense here, as in the Borough, of easy wealth and of leisurely living. The poverty of the city affects the ability of the school district to hire good teachers, and it also erodes the ability of parents to provide a culturally nurturing environment for their children. Some enter the local illegal economy of drugs, and some end up in prison or get murdered. Because the physical landscape has been allowed to become eroded by shopkeepers who fled to the new mall outside town or by landlords who have no incentive to invest their earnings in maintaining the buildings they own, the feel of many parts of the city is depressing. The vitality that one feels in a commercial culture of small shops in a place like Mystic is not present, and few people other than the homeless and the unemployed are to be seen on the streets during the day. One of the busiest parts of town is the Court House where small claims cases are heard, a symptom of an economic situation in which scarce resources lead to fights over their distribution.

While a landscape can be read as a text and interpreted for its embedded meanings, it is also a place where power relations assume physical existence. Beyond Mystic, further out into the water, is Mason's Island. It was the reward given to John Mason, the man who led the massacre of the Pequots. A few middle-class people live there, but mostly it is the home of doctors and owners of car dealerships and landscape architects. It is a place of great physical beauty; the houses are far apart and all well designed; it is hugged by the water on all sides. The experience of being there can be a relief from the Mystic crowds. But it is a gated community. Not everyone is allowed to enter, and a guard gate keeps out those who do not have an "M" on their windscreen. That exclusion and that "exclusiveness" foster a sense of being in a community of equally wealthy people apart from the common lot. One can count on one's friends to be roughly in the same income bracket as oneself, especially at the yacht club where so much of the island's community life occurs. That personal feeling embodies what are called *class relations*, the difference between social groups as that is tallied by wealth held and income earned. By controlling the pricing and wage-setting mechanism of the unregulated market economy, the wealthy inhabitants of the island assure that they will take more of the total social resources than others. Those others in turn will have to make do with less income and live in places that are much less beautiful – in Mystic or the local "poor white trash" countryside or New London. It is simply a part of the structure of things or a feature of the way society operates that differences of economic power register as geographic differences.

Student Exercise

You all live in different, quite varied places, so it would be hard if not impossible to come up with a single suggestion for a practical exercise you might perform based on the ideas of Cultural Geography.

Look around where you live and try to find some aspect of the built environment that interests you or that strikes you as an especially good example of a distinct social place, building, or landscape.

Malls are always fun to analyze, but in addition to the usual "reading" of the building and the activities that take place within, you might investigate what the effect of the building of the mall had on local shopping habits and previous shopping areas. Where I live, the building of the Crystal Mall outside New London in 1984 had a very negative effect on the downtown of the city. Local merchants could no longer compete with the department store chains such as Macys that could buy in bulk for lower prices and in turn sell for lower prices to customers. New London is now a ghost town, and the mall is a thriving commercial center.

But less obvious examples are available. Where I live as well, it's possible to analyze the changing cultural significance of the countryside around the new Pequot mega-casino, which was built on a reservation that was initially chosen by whites because the land had so little value: it was a swamp. But now the new casino stands in the middle of North Stonington, a charming, bucolic town with pastures, woods, and farms.

Finally, urban change is always interesting to consider. I work in Philadelphia, a largely African American city. But its real estate, especially the areas where blacks live, is becoming increasingly valuable, and white real estate developers are "gentrifying" the black areas, buying dilapidated houses and refurbishing them for sale to the wealthy. Gentrification changes the landscape. How and why the change occurs indicate something about those changing it. Are there similar changes happening near you, and how do you read or interpret them?

Sources

Regarding landscapes, see D. W. Meining, ed., *The Interpretation of Ordinary Landscape* (New York, 1979). Regarding cultural geography, see Alison Blunt, ed., *Cultural Geography in Practice* (London, 2003); William Norton, *Cultural Geography: Themes, Concepts, Analyses* (Don Mills, Ont., 2000); Don Mitchell, *Cultural Geography: A Critical Introduction* (Malden, Mass., 2000); Kenneth Foote, ed., *Re-Reading Cultural Geography* (Austin, Tex., 1994); P. Cloke and R. Johnston (eds.), *Spaces in Geographical Thought* (London, 2005); and P. Jackson, *Maps of Meaning: An Introduction to Cultural Geography* (London, 1994).

3

Gender and Sexuality

Gender is a mix of nature and culture, of biology and learned behavior. At the grocery checkout counter in North America, for example, one is more likely to encounter magazines with physically attractive women adorning the covers than men. The faces in such images possess a symmetry that is not simply aesthetic; biologists argue such symmetry is associated in men's unconscious minds with a greater possibility of reproductive success. Culture would seem, therefore, to have a natural basis. But our gender lives also have a social dimension; those images of women on magazine covers are more likely to be seen by the women who in most societies are charged with the labor of shopping. It is a culturally designated women's task. Savvy producers of magazines know what their audience is and where to find them. But even this qualification can be said to return us to nature – to, in this instance, the drive to accumulate resources for oneself as a means of survival. And since men possess more of those resources than women and have access more readily to them than do women, the magazine culture of sexual attractiveness could be read as having to do with the need women feel to make themselves attractive to men with power over resources in a world in which those resources are inequitably and unevenly distributed between and amongst the genders. Women's survival may depend on beauty. If you go online, you will find sites devoted to Sugar Daddies (such as SeekingArrangement.com), who look for younger women to support financially in exchange for sexual favors, but few if any sites for women endowed with similar economic, social, and sexual power.

Culture thus can express nature in many ways. But in recent years, scholars of culture have also explored the ways in which culture shapes nature.

Our biological gender usually expresses itself in cultural forms such as dress and hairstyle in a way that might convince us that gender identity is entirely a matter of biological destiny whose most palpable physical emblem is our differing genitalia. We see expressions of gender nature everywhere, from women's birthing of babies to men's usually larger bodies, and those expressions are consistent over time. Women in ancient times wore dresses and looked after children, and they still do so today in many places. But sociologists argue that much of the behavior that is considered natural to a gender identity is in fact taught and learned. The pressure of the social power hierarchy, for example, which favors men over women in economic and political life, imprints on women dispositions that may favor the reproduction over time of that hierarchy. The seemingly spontaneous and natural desire many young women feel in conservative social locations especially to become caretakers of men and of children may not be spontaneously generated at all. It may be a lesson learned from the surrounding culture that was placed there by men because their own interests were served by it. And the imprinting of those ideals and norms on women makes the existing gender power relations appear to arise spontaneously from a natural process – women seem to spontaneously want to engage in service labor for men – but in fact, those internal dispositions toward certain kinds of behavior are learned. They seem original, but they are repetitions, rote rehearsals of scripts whose scripted character has been erased or forgotten.

What appears to be nature, in other words, may be a fabrication. It may be culture.

Similarly, sexuality, which might be called the practice of gender, would seem to be characterized by a clear male-female binary opposition in most people. Biology would seem to sustain a limited dyadic heterosexual paradigm or model. But sexuality is so forged by culture and experience and so bent from the simple dominant heterosexual binary in plural ways that it in fact consists of a fluid range of possibilities – even in those firmly lodged in one of the binary heterosexual identities. In the Japanese "queerscape" on the Internet, for example, adult women, many of whom, one can probably assume, are heterosexual, explore their fascination with adult male–boy homosexuality. The dominant binary opposition would seem to prescribe a matching scheme of desired objects – women for men, men for women. But many people turn away from that simple choice and seek other possibilities, and within each of the principle heterosexual choices, there are multiple ways to practice sexuality, each determined by, in all likelihood, a mix of biological and experiential influences. Some take pleasure in being "femme" and passive, while other enjoy being "butch" and dominant. Within the heterosexual majority, those different iterations or forms of sexuality tend to be obscured. The categorical norm of male-female makes us think everyone in the majority practices the same hetero-sexuality. But, of course, that is not the case. Some heterosexual women have what the culture calls strong "masculine" traits, while others prefer less assertive approaches to gender identity and to sexuality. And the same range can be found in men, between active and passive, assertive and recep-tive, and so on. We are many things sexually.

When one takes gay and lesbian experience into account, the simplicity of gender and sexuality is also challenged. Add bisexuality, and things become more complex. Moreover, around the world, people unhappy with the physical gender nature assigned them dress the part of the gender they prefer, and they can have surgery that transforms them into a manufac-tured version of the natural gender they would have preferred. Some people enjoy multiple forms of sexuality, both heterosexual and homosexual; they make the socially normative injunction that one has to be choosy seem overly restrictive. The gay-lesbian-bisexual-transsexual challenge to heter-onormativity is not limited to noting that alternatives exist; it also strikes at the way the norm operates to curtail and repress multiple possibilities and multiple sexual desires within heterosexual identity itself. Scholars of sexuality have found that most people's desires are not limited to the privi-leged heterosexual object assigned to his or her identity within the hetero-sexual matrix. Many heterosexual men feel desire at some point in their lives for other men, and the same is true of heterosexual women.

Nevertheless, a study of gender and sexuality in human culture reminds us that culture is also nature. Humans may fabricate cultural lessons regarding appropriate gender identity that conditions or determines how future generations of young people are trained to behave (boys learn never to wear dresses in most cultures), but each human being is a physical machine programmed by genetics and propelled by chemicals. Some of the interesting complexity of gender culture and some of the most compelling problems of gender identity arise at those points where physical drives confront cultural norms. Lesbian women, for example, who could not imagine being heterosexual for perfectly natural reasons, found themselves in the past stigmatized because they did not embrace the gender norms of the cultures in which they lived. All human cultures are dominated by heterosexual men and by the social imperatives that seem to be the cultural legacy of their biological reality. Fear of homosexuality and especially of female homosexuality has been a consistent feature of male heterosexual culture over time. Strong "masculine" women are portrayed as Medusas or witches who harm men. Only in recent years have lesbian women been accepted at least in some cultural regions. In others, women are still expected to be passive and subservient, and signs of independence and strength, such as wishing to choose one's own spouse, are punished, oftentimes violently. In South Asia, hundreds of women are murdered or mutilated each year for disobeying male relatives and "dishonoring" them.

In studying the culture of gender and sexuality, we necessarily explore a realm of oftentimes troubling and occasionally dangerous feelings. It is also a realm of power, where groups subordinate other groups along gender lines and in terms of access to the resource of sexuality. But gender and sexuality have always also been areas of enormous human creativity and play, where both the natural drive to reproduce humanity and the urge toward pleasure through and with others are on display.

The cultural realm of gender and sexuality extends from deep within the human mind to billboards and television commercials that exist in communal public spaces. The constant along that range is the way affect and image are welded together in human experience both within the private realm of cognition and in the public realm of cultural representation. What ends up on the billboards and the commercials is what is deeply felt by us. And what is most deeply felt is a mix of chemistry and image. The mind works by translating feelings into images in cognition. That explains why cultural images, especially those dealing with profound feelings of the kind that are linked to gender and sexuality, can have such a strong effect on us. Those images evoke powerful feelings because they are linked in their creators' minds to profound feelings. As much as represent real men or women, they give expression to inner feelings and emotional states. All of this helps explain why culture is in a sense nature. Genetically determined biological and chemical processes express themselves in our minds as words and images that bear affect and communicate feelings from the physical realm into the mental and cultural one. Mental images are thus like gateways that conduct non-mental processes and states into the realm of cognition and conscious awareness. When those images are made public, they become our culture, and in our culture, images of men and women and of sexuality especially can move us profoundly because of their origins in our deepest selves. Images of sexually attractive men and women's bodies elicit sexual desire because they are already embedded with such desire.

Horror movies, for example, are a form of cultural imagery embedded with emotion. They evoke powerful feelings and are often characterized by highly sexual, gendered imagery. One did not have to be a trained scholar of culture to notice that the film *Alien* (1979) dealt with male anxieties about female sexuality. Trapped in a space ship run by "Mother," a dangerous and coldhearted computer, the space workers are killed one by one by a vicious creature whose head resembles an erect penis and which turns men into women by birthing itself out of their bodies. Danger first appears in an egg hatchery and is linked to female reproduction when the alien seed, having been planted in one of the men through the mouth, erupts from his stomach in an image resembling birth. The man is turned into a woman, a recurring image in cultural stories about male sexual fears. Fear of not being masculine, of not attaining a sexual identity that matches male heterosexual norms, often takes the imagistic form of either masculine women or feminine men. Women who are masculine provoke fear in men because they do not match the heterosexual norm for women. If men are supposed to be active and dominant in that cultural paradigm, women are supposed to be passive and subordinate. Images of powerful women in horror films therefore often imply male anxieties regarding masculinity failure. At the time the film was made, in the 1970s, the feminist movement was transforming traditional heterosexual gender norms and relations. Women were becoming more assertive personally and publicly, abandoning roles that had been taken to be natural. In that climate, it would be understandable that men might begin to feel that their own identities had become less fixed, stable, or natural seeming.

But there is also a deeper psychological dimension to male fear. A cold and insufficiently caring mother might provoke in a boy a sense of dislocation regarding his gender identity and his sexuality. Without some sense of confirming affection, he might take the world to be a threatening place. Without an internal monitor for his emotions that is derived from early experiences of care by others, he might not be able to control his feelings in regard to sexuality especially, an area that demands that one relate to others in a particular way. His gender identity might not develop toward the heterosexual norm he sees endorsed all around him in his culture. Women might come to appear "monstrous," and his sexual drives, because they are not encouraged, become instead repressed. Repression tends to force material that might flow freely into a compressed form that can increase its force. Sexuality as a result can become violent, and that violence can be directed against women who, as emblems of the cold mother, are perceived to be the source of one's sexual blockage and gender fear. In "real life" this failure of care and self-development can lead to someone like Ted

Bundy, who killed numerous young women all of whom resembled a girl-friend who rejected him. Because he was illegitimate, his mother pretended to be his sister as he grew up, so he had no one to care for him and to nurture a healthy gendered self in which affect could be monitored internally. Instead, it repeatedly erupted in rage and violence.

Movies monsters are often expressions of similar emotions. They tear people apart after all, just like serial killers. The monster in *Alien* poses an interesting problem of gender identity because it is both masculine and feminine, and its confusion is an index of the instability of gender identity that motivates the film's fantasy story. The monster embodies a boy's fear of female sexuality as something so powerful that it makes it impossible for him to achieve certification as a heterosexual male. If women are powerful and active, it means men are passive and weak. The monster also embodies a boy's fears regarding the violent power of his sexual drives. The coldhearted "Mother" is at the root of the problem both in the story of the film and in "real life." And the solution – in the film and perhaps in real life world of male heterosexual fantasy – is for a woman to quell the monstrous violence of sexuality by adopting a feminine posture appropriate to the heterosexual norm the film's narrative ultimately seeks to re-establish. Ripley, the female lead, becomes a caring mother who looks after her cat, and she strips almost naked in a display of sexual attractiveness that repositions women as sexual certifiers of normative male heterosexual identity. They cease to resemble a cold, uncaring Mother and become visual emblems of realized male desire for attentive care and sexual pleasure.

These cultural images should be seen as expressions of the chemistry of life, as further iterations of what really goes on in human psychological development and in human interaction. If monster movies seem irrational, it is because elements of our lives together, when not conducted with care, can become highly irrational.

Culture also consists of stories about our lives, and all of us live our life stories as gendered creatures. The stories or narratives that tell our lives are often themselves gendered, from the "hard-boiled" detective genre of the 1930s on in America, which was a heavily masculine literary form in which men learned to be strong to survive in a tough world, to the "chick lit" of the 1990s, which depicted female experience and was more concerned with struggles against personal failure and with striving for success in relating to others effectively. Such cultural stories change with time. The masculine stories were written at a time when men were the designated breadwinners for families, and competition for scarce resources imposed on them an ideal of toughness as a mechanism for assuring survival in a harsh economic landscape. Concomitantly, the chick-lit phenomenon arguably appealed to young women who belonged to a generation unleashed for the first time in human history from traditional strictures on women. More independent sexually and self-sufficient economically than their mothers or ancestors, they faced a more precarious and risky social universe in which the quest for a mate involved new forms of cultural negotiation and placed one in contact with a wider range of possible partners. In the older world of masculine toughness and female wile, roles were more staged and predictable. In the new world of post-feminist life, scripts often had to be written on the run, and the behavior of others was as a consequence less predictable. To an extent, Bridget Jones' life is as adventurous, as much a matter of questing to get the right answer to a life puzzle, as the life of Sam Spade or the Continental Op.

Not all cultural narratives are as benign as the Bridget Jones story. And not all women live in social universes characterized by such freedom of action or such choices as Bridget faces. In Africa, women living within traditional gender cultures are more likely to be victimized by AIDS because a culture of safe sex does not exist. You are very unlikely in your lives to see stories dealing with such issues. You might see a movie called *Quartier Mozart* from Cameroon that depicts a young woman's attempt to deal with the male culture of cavalier sexuality, but it is unlikely. Moreover, for every cute White Bridget in America, there are scores of young African American women whose lives are limited by economic pressures. These life stories do not make for popular cultural fare; they are snagged by the filters that assure that the stories we consume most commonly are pleasurable rather than disturbing. Works of literature can deal with such harsh realities because they do not require enormous amounts of money to produce and can therefore get by with less income from a smaller consumer base. Film and television, however, are expensive cultural products, so they must appeal broadly to a large population to guarantee a return on investment. They cannot risk creating pain rather than pleasure. A comparison of a successful television show about gender with a recent novel bears out this point.

Sex and the City was a popular television show in the US that ran from 1998 to 2004 on Home Box Office (HBO). That venue was less dependent on commercials for financing and so was less constrained by the need to stay within the bounds of the current standards for public morality. It permitted the producers of *SATC* to challenge the boundaries for representations of single women's gender and sexual issues. The dialog was frankly sexual, and the show also explored new terrain by depicting young single women whose professional success afforded them a much wider range of choices regarding sexual and romantic partners than would have been possible for women a half century earlier in America. The show both registered a significant cultural change and was itself an agent of such change. That it was created and produced by gay men added an element of gender complexity to the representation of the young women's lives. The show often recalled the norm-challenging excess that in the past was to be found in such popular cultural forms in gay male culture as burlesque, disco, and camp.

Prior to the contemporary era, the traditional format for heterosexual mating was male pursuit and female acquiescence, with men winning bread while women stayed home and baked it. The economic world sustained that paradigm by permitting men access to wealth and denying access to women. That economic structure and those cultural practices have begun to change, although even in newly developed and supposedly "advanced" economic cultures such as Ireland, the list of wealthiest people in the new economy is still entirely male. Nevertheless, marriage is less attractive for many people than it was a generation or so ago; 55 percent of men are married, down from 69.3 percent in 1960, and 51.5 percent of women are, down from 65.9 percent in 1960.

SATC depicts a new world in which women have economic power (to a certain limited degree) and as a result have greater leverage in negotiating a life format with possible mates. In such a new gender world, the traditional marriage and parenting format can be treated with skepticism, as in an episode entitled "The Baby Shower," in which the four female friends at the center of the show are depicted exhibiting disdain for married life. Nevertheless, for all of its adventurousness, the show's driving narrative force was the quest for the right mate. In one episode ("Attack of the Five Foot Ten Woman"), two characters obsess over the marriages section in the city newspaper. In the movie made of the show, the main character, Carrie, when she is about to marry her appropriately named mate "Big," goes through her wardrobe throwing out clothes that represent parts of her self that no longer "count" as her in her new role in life. Even as it explores the detachability of sex from reproduction, *SATC* reminds us that the physical machinery of sex is in fact inseparable from reproduction and from the cultural institutions such as marriage and family that humans have built up around that natural fact.

SATC's commitment to the dominant model of heterosexual marriage for the sake of family-formation is not unqualified, however. One character decides in the movie version to do without her boyfriend because she prefers life on her own terms, and in the episode entitled "They Shoot Single People Don't They?" the girls decide it is better to live alone than with the wrong mate. Hedging all of the series' exploration of new era single women's lives is the obdurate economic reality of male wealth and comparable female poverty. Men largely control the economic world and possess the power that goes with it, and in the New York metropolitan area, the setting for the series, single women outnumber single men by 770,000, turning the city into a male sexual shopping mall. The series and the movie bump up against those realities occasionally, as when Big in the movie buys Carrie an apartment that probably cost millions of dollars. However much the show challenges traditional notions regarding women and sexuality, it accepts and even endorses that basic gender power relation. In *SATC*, men rule and young women drool, as the Middle School rhyme goes. And it is difficult to locate the line where the natural and the cultural ingredients of that reality separate – if they do at all.

Novels can go much deeper than a popular television show, even a supposedly less commercial one, in exploring issues related to gender and sexuality. A case in point is Natsuo Kirino's novel *Real World* (2008), which concerns Japanese high school girls who become involved with a boy named Worm who has murdered his mother. One of them helps him, and they both die in a car crash as the police pursue them. Plot aside, the novel really concerns gender identity and how boys and girls both are conditioned and respond inventively to their conditioning by adopting various roles or performing different, almost theatrical, gender parts in their engagement with others. One of the girls is lesbian, dresses like a tomboy, and speaks in a low voice to imitate a man. Another is an ultra-feminine Barbie Girl, who dyes her hair blonde, modifies her body by going to tanning salons to turn her skin light brown, and uses glue in her eyelashes so that they permanently curl up. She does this in order to be "totally accepted." Her extreme role forms a continuity with the more "normal" roles that the other girls perform that underscore the daily, ritualized basis of gender identity and performance: "She answered the phone in that cutesy, friendly voice she reserves for phone calls."

The novel also focuses on gender gray areas that fall outside of or between the standard heterosexual model. There are older men who molest young girls on trains and transvestites who resent the presence of lesbian girls in their neighborhood of the city and beat them up:

> Boku-chan was trying her best to become a guy. … Boku-chan had the single fixed idea that, since she liked women, she wanted to become a nice man, and that in order to become one, she needed to act manly. Which to her meant frowning as you held your cigarette between thumb and forefinger, putting your arm around a girl's shoulder and lifting her chin with your finger, speaking in a deep, threatening voice, adopting all the poses and actions of hunky actors in movies. She was tall, had studied karate, and was muscular, so she had the mannerisms down, but somehow when she did it, it all came off as a joke.[1]

Worm, the murderer, is a victim of gendered cultural conditioning. Badgered by his mother to perform well in cram school, his sexuality has become bent from physical expression and become focused on women's undergarments and voyeurism. His solution is violence and the adoption of a militaristic role that he performs with one of the high school girls, by enlisting her as a subordinate.

The Internet has become an important cultural and political tool for members of minority gender and sexual groups. It allows easy access to public discussion and news broadcasting by those without access to radio or television stations or networks. On such sites as http://www.queerty. com, information can be disseminated, issues discussed, and political action taken in a way that is not possible in mainstream media outlets.[2] The entries on Queerty for October 9, 2008, for example, concerned television commercials that aimed to convince people to stop using gay-derogatory expressions such as "That's so gay!" It also reports on an effort in Canada to question the judgment of a minister who allowed a gay-hating African singer to enter the country. Buju Banton sings songs in which he urges listeners to murder gays. If one goes to the Queerty Japan site, one can find a link to AfterEllen.com, a site for lesbians. There, for the same day, a poll asks viewers to vote for the best lesbian kiss on television, but the discussion framing the vote notes that such kisses are often aimed at a heterosexual audience and often appear in episodes timed to coincide with award voting:

> Lesbians get blamed for a lot of things, from the destruction of the nuclear family to the death of traditional values, but no one can deny lesbians are good for one thing, at least: boosting TV ratings during the critical "sweeps" periods of the year (November, February and May), when audience size, later used to set advertising rates, is measured.[3]

Gay culture is thriving on the Net, but gays remain targets of homophobic taunting and bullying in schools around the world. In a study of Massachusetts schools in the US, for example, 97 percent of the students reported hearing homophobic remarks from fellow students at their school; 53 percent reported hearing such remarks from school staff. The negative consequences of such an atmosphere in which the culture licenses homophobia are worth noting. In the same Massachusetts school system, gay and lesbian students were four times more likely to report being threatened with physical violence. Mental health professionals have conducted studies that show that homophobia in schools results in self-harm and the internalization of homophobia among gay men. Perhaps in consequence gay and lesbian adolescents are up to four times more likely to commit suicide than their peers. As many as 40 percent of homosexual adolescents attempt suicide. In Japan where demands to conform are more pronounced in the culture, homosexuals experience shame and guilt because they do not fit the heteronormative standards of society. The guilt has less to do with being gay per se than with not fitting the norms of their society. Cultural homophobia is therefore linked to cultural heteronormativity. And television shows like *SATC* are part of the problem. The media has moved beyond portraying gays as deviants who usually ended up dead or symbolically demoted at the conclusion of the narrative, but these days, gays are still more likely to be portrayed in patronizing ways. Gay men in *SATC* are more often than not associated with fashion tips and cheeky one-liners rather than be depicted as full humans, like the girls on the show, who face an uphill battle in surviving in a culture dominated by heterosexual men and their imperatives.

Student Exercise

One of the most interesting ideas regarding gender to emerge in Cultural Studies contends that our gender identities are performances, like theatrical performances on stage. We act out ideals of gender identity such as "femininity" and "masculinity" that would not appear normally or naturally in the absence of strong cultural and social pressures on us to perform or act in certain ways. For this exercise, watch the film *Paris Is Burning*, a documentary about gay males who like to dress up in costumes and compete with each other in "balls" in New York City. The film at points suggests that "straight" culture is itself based on costume wearing. Straight heterosexuals perform gender roles that give them identity; they do not express a natural gender identity in their clothes.

Is this true? To what extent is gender rule-bound?

In the movie *Mean Girls*, Cady Heron is an American teenager living in the US for the first time, who learns that "Having lunch with The Plastics was like leaving the actual world and entering 'Girl World'. And Girl World had a lot of rules." You might read *The Rules: Time-Tested Secrets for Capturing the Heart of Mr. Right* by Ellen Fein and Sherrie Schneider, which was a self-help dating manual released in 1995. It was a word-of-mouth bestseller that started an entire franchise. The book advocated a return to more "old-fashioned" dating practices, such as the following: "No more than casual kissing on the first date" and "Don't accept a Saturday night date after Wednesday." The Rules instruct women to not talk too much, to never tell a man what to do, to always end phone calls first, and to not rush into sex. Are women really like what the Rules portray women as needing to be in order to "get" a man? Why do women have to worry and think about "getting" a man? To what extent are such gender roles learned, and to what extent natural?

Sex and the City, the movie based on the popular TV show, begins with Carrie Bradshaw, the main character and sex columnist, saying, "Year after year, 20-something women come to New York City in search of the two L's: Labels and love. Twenty years ago, I was one of them. Having gotten the knack for labels early, I concentrated on my search for love. Turns out, a knockoff is not as easy to spot when it comes to love." The movie ends with her saying,

Maybe some labels are best left in the closet. Maybe when we label people: "Bride," "groom," "husband," "wife," "married," "single," we forget to look past the label to the person. And there, in the same city where they met as girls, four New York women entered the next phase of their lives dressed head to toe in love. And that's the one label that never goes out of style.

Discuss these statements in relation to the clothes-changing sequences in the movie. How does clothing function as a metaphor for love in the movie?

Finally, discuss the *SATC* phenomenon in relation to the following. Women are socialized from a very early age to consider and prioritize other people's feelings. They are socialized to perceive emotional connection in relationships as extremely valuable. In fact, women's identities are often largely defined through their relationships with others and their capacity to nurture these loved ones. This socialization often engenders the development of strong relationship and intimacy-building skills in women, which serve as a bridge to intimacy. On the other hand, this focus on relationships can become a barrier to achieving intimacy if it precludes attention to individual needs. Traditional gender socialization may result in some women having difficulty with prioritizing self-care, championing their own needs, and developing aspects of identity that are separate from others – all of which are important to the capacity to intimately connect with another person. Many scholars have noted that male socialization involves a degree of suppression of emotional expression and vulnerability which may make it difficult for some men to feel comfortable with or develop skills in emotional expression, self-disclosure, and interpersonal vulnerability. Male socialization also involves an expectation that men are highly sexual. They are encouraged to view women as sex objects, pressured to engage in sex at an early age, and taught to use sex as a way to validate their masculinity. Male socialization involves a view of sex as satisfactory when divorced from emotional connection. Some argue that this socialization leads some men to sexualize feelings of emotional or non-sexual closeness and to focus on the physical aspects of sexuality to the preclusion of emotional or relationship aspects. These social expectations may also lead some men to equate their personal worth with their sexual performance, virility, and ability to attract and please a partner.

Notes

1. Natsuo Kirino, *Real World* (New York, 2008).
2. Queerty, "Queerty: Free of an Agenda. Except That Gay One," http://www.queerty.com (accessed October 8, 2009).
3. Christie Keith, "Top 10 Moments in Sweeps Lesbianism," AfterEllen.com, November 14, 2006, http://www.afterellen.com/archive/ellen/TV/2006/11/sweeps.html (accessed October 8, 2009).

Sources

On gender and sexuality, see Roger Lancaster and Micaela di Leonardo, *The Gender/Sexuality Reader: Culture, History, Political Economy* (New York, 1997); Richard Parker, Regina Maria Barbosa, and Peter Aggleton, *Framing the Sexual Subject: The Politics of Gender, Sexuality, and Power* (Berkeley, Calif., 2000); and Mary Holmes, *Gender in Everyday Life* (New York, 2009). On sexual harassment, see Elizabeth Meyer, *Gender, Bullying, and Harassment: Strategies to End Sexism and Homophobia in Schools* (New York, 2009); and Massachusetts Governor's Commission on Gay and Lesbian Youth, *Making Schools Safe for Gay and Lesbian Youth: Breaking the Silence in Schools and in Families* (Boston, 1993).

4

Ideologies

The word *ideology* has several meanings in Cultural Studies. An ideology is a body of ideas that license, enable, and direct social action. The ideology of racism, for example, provides a coherent set of beliefs and reasons that justify social or physical violence against another ethnic group. The arguments and word images in the ideology portray the other ethnic group as lacking qualities that would make them meritorious, qualities supposedly present in the racist group. For example, some conservative Whites in the United States vilify other ethnic groups such as African Americans and Hispanics. The Whites portray themselves as hardworking and industrious and portray Blacks and Hispanics as lazy freeloaders who steal jobs from Whites or who oblige Whites to support them through government assistance funded by taxation imposed on Whites.

Ideology also refers to mistaken cognition that prevents us from seeing reality as it is. Ideology in this sense describes the way social groups who have over-accumulated economic resources maintain their power by imposing on society frames of understanding and perception that prevent the true nature of the society from being seen and discussed. For example, we are taught to perceive ourselves as "individuals" in American culture rather than as members of an economic class, and as a result, we have a difficult time seeing society in terms of relations between economic groups. The fact that one small group over-accumulates social wealth can thus be portrayed as the result of "individual initiative" instead of being seen as a manifestation of a class structure. Any attempt to draw attention to such realities will be branded "class warfare" and dunned in the right-wing media as inappropriate speech that is outside the "mainstream."

Ideology also consists of what are called "ruling ideas". These are ideas that ruling social groups force into a position of centrality in a culture. The ideas generally reinforce the power of the ruling group by making their rule or their claim on social wealth seem natural, legitimate, and uncontestable. For several centuries, social groups that have laid claim to excess social resources have used the ideas *freedom* and *liberty* to justify such inequality. In its most recent iteration or incarnation, the ideology of freedom fostered the belief fairly widely around the world that markets should be unregulated by governments. This, of course, was tantamount to walking into a playground in which a small group of rowdy bullies had been prevented from lording it over everyone else by school rules and announcing, "No holds barred. It's a free-for-all." In such a scenario, the weaker would suffer; the bullies would use their physical advantage in sheer force to dominate everyone else. The way the ideology of freedom played out did not mimic this scenario exactly. Lots of people around the globe jumped on the bandwagon and thrived economically – but always by taking advantage of others' poverty and comparative weakness in "free" labor markets to generate a huge amount of wealth for themselves.

Ideologies are usually held by groups of people with a particular interest that is served by the ideology. Ideologies provide explanations that make the world seem more easily understandable, and usually the explanations are self-serving. Ideologies usually are inaccurate and unscientific. They often mix non-rational forms of thinking with mistaken interpretations of the world. In the case of the White conservative racist ideology regarding African Americans, the mistake consists of thinking an effect or result of racism is a justification for racism. One of the crucial operations of ideology is to turn effects into causes. The process goes like this: race-based discrimination has over time deprived African Americans of access to economic power. As a result, many African Americans in the US have been pushed into poverty, and poverty, when persistent over time and from generation to generation, produces a sense of disillusion and disaffection. That sense of disaffection can reduce initiative because effort seems not to guarantee results. But that lack of initiative, instead of being seen as an effect of racism, is seen as the cause that accounts for economic failure. And this justifies the claim that African Americans lack talents and abilities of the sort that would bring them wealth. An effect of discrimination – such as disaffection, a lack of initiative, or the absence of a sense of economic purpose – becomes a reason or cause for discrimination in the minds of conservatives. The group practicing racist discourse thus justifies their own greater access to economic resources by making others appear less deserving.

Ideology also refers to mistaken cognition that helps secure the subordination of poor people to a wealthy and politically powerful economic elite. The elite, as part of their economic power, control the mechanisms of cultural production such as television and newspapers that provide the filters and frames through which many people view the world. The owners of the filters control what will be seen or how reality will be perceived. This sense of the word *ideology* places more emphasis on the way poor people who often lack training in critical-thinking skills as a result of underfunded education are led to perceive the world in ways that go against their own economic interests and serve the interests of those with wealth and power in a society. During the 2008 presidential election campaign in the US, for example, it was noteworthy that poor uneducated voters had their thinking easily changed by rumors and advertisements that were clearly false (assertions that Barack Obama was a Muslim) or that sought to distract attention from issues dangerous to the agenda of the wealthy (the persistence of extreme economic inequality, for example) by labeling any discussion of such issues as *socialism*. The ideological discourse also shifted attention to pre-rational issues such as "blood-lines." At the same time, CNN, a network that generally fosters ideology rather than critical-thinking skills, sought to convince its audience that immigrants were the cause of the economic crisis facing the country – not extreme economic inequality or an unregulated financial sector. By picturing the world in a certain way for audiences, the culture industries shape what will and what will not be seen. They construct reality for their consumers, and that picture of reality is usually inaccurate. It treats essential structural problems such as economic inequality as accidental side effects of otherwise rational social, economic, and political processes.

Cultural ideas are clearly not just ideas. They have force, and they can change how we think about the world. Our ideas are not all our own. We learn ideas in school, from our family culture, from our peers, from books that we read, and from the media. Culture courses through our brains as the ideas that flash upon he screens of our consciousness. Some of those thoughts we fabricate ourselves, but some of them follow forms and formats given to us by our culture. Those ideas can color how we perceive the world. It has become almost routine in the US, for example, for *Arab* and *terrorist* to be joined in the popular imagination. Seldom do Americans see in the media fully rounded characters of Arab descent who are not portrayed as dangers. Too, because of a successful cultural campaign by those who benefit from strict free market capitalism over the past several decades in the US, it is impossible to hear anything positive about socialism (a popular social and economic approach in Europe and elsewhere) in the US context. You will never see a television show about the virtues of socialism in the US media in part because the media are owned and controlled by people whose interests would be hurt by the socialist ideal of an equitable distribution of wealth and in part because the dominant way of thinking in the culture is so opposed to socialism as a result of repeated instruction over many decades from those with economic and cultural power. Even if the message were broadcast, in other words, it could not be heard.

If ideas shape consciousness, consciousness shapes behavior. A Marine is not just a person in a uniform; Marines are people who have learned a particular way of behaving by absorbing particular ideas (rules, values, ideals, models of behavior, etc.) that shape who they are and determine how they act in the world. The term we use for the distinct kind of self that the term Marine embodies is *identity*. An identity is one thing rather than another; it is a differentiation between two things. By absorbing one set of ideas, values, and ideals, a Marine becomes a particular identity that is NOT something else. To be a Marine is to be tough rather than weak, for example, capable of killing rather than reflective on the ethical implications of violence. You could take the cluster of qualities a Marine is NOT and make out of them an identity antithetical to that of the Marine – someone with a doctorate in philosophy who is a strict pacifist, for example.

This explains why in at least one school of thought in Cultural Studies, *ideology* refers both to the ideas that circulate in a particular culture and to the kinds of self-identity that those ideas make possible. Cultures differ from each other across the globe in the way that they foster different kinds of self-identity. Different ideas make us into different kinds of people. People around the world differ and have different kinds of identity because cultures differ in regard to the kinds of ideas that dominate in each culture. To study cultural difference is often to study the ways large groups of people are managed and directed by the dominant ideas of that culture to have particular kinds of identity that make that particular society work in a particular way.

In the US, a culture that has already moved away from traditional village-based cultural and social forms, young people are encouraged to think of themselves increasingly as active agents who have full control over their lives. That is an important break with the previous patriarchal tradition that held that they should be carefully supervised. In China, by contrast, a culture still steeped in traditional ideas and values, young women from rural areas who migrate to cities for work in factories are encouraged to think of themselves as *dagonmei*, dutiful and obedient daughters who substitute the factory boss for their older brothers and fathers. The rural patriarchal tradition of obedience for young women is thus adapted to the new industrial economic order in China.

The idea (and personal ideal) that dominates in America is *freedom* for reasons that have to do with how particular social and economic groups pressed their case and their self-interest most successfully throughout US history; the ideal that dominates the lives of young women in newly industrial China is "obedience" for reasons that have to do with the wishes of the ruling political elite to foster greater economic productivity that will raise China out of poverty and make it a modern industrial nation. If in the US, the common good is sacrificed for self-interest, in China, self-interest serves the common good. Different dominant ideas and ideals mold identities differently in each place.

History also provides examples of the way ideologies change over time. Prior to the invention of liberalism, the body of ideas associated with political democracy and the idea of personal or individual freedom, most European societies were characterized by ideas that sustained an authoritarian social model founded on hierarchy and obedience. Under feudalism, the dominant ideas were not freedom or democracy but duty and loyalty. And people thought of themselves differently as a result. Peasants did not think they were free to choose amongst a variety of possible life paths. Their place in life was established for them by their society, and their culture, largely religious, convinced them that their duty was to stay in their place and to perform their assigned tasks. The dominant cultural idea had it that society was a corporate, organic whole in which each part performed its role. The age of liberalism or of personal freedom founded on the idea of the individual operates according to a different picture of the world. Individuals move about freely if they can in the economic network. But some would argue such free movement and action only reinforces rigid social structures by making them appear more flexible than they actually are. Even as one moves up the class ladder, it remains a class ladder, and one's efforts only make it all the more rational, normal, and acceptable as a way of arranging our world. By freely choosing which consumer goods to buy, we merely tie more tightly the chains that prevent genuine freedom from coming into being by fostering an economic system organized around enforced labor for the majority so that a minority can enjoy excess wealth.

In studying ideology in culture, then, there are several strands of inquiry that one can pursue. One concerns ideas that become the bases of social action. An example, in the US in recent years, would be the way evangelical Christianity has provided undereducated people with an ideational justification for pre-modern attitudes toward race, gender, and sexuality. "Old time religion" – a particular selection of biblical quotes – thus becomes the basis for a drive to turn back modernity.

Religion is probably the most obvious example of an ideology defined as a group of ideas that seem coherent but that foster misperceptions and misrepresentations of the world. Evangelicalism has achieved a place of prominence in popular culture in recent decades, abetted in part by political leaders like George W. Bush. Timothy LaHave's *Left Behind* novels and movies, for example, were extremely popular. In the first book in the *Left Behind* series, *Rapture*, the taking of true believers to heaven by God, happens suddenly, and those "left behind," who have not achieved perfect salvation, must do battle with the Anti-Christ in order to save the world. In *Left Behind*, those actually left on earth are portrayed as not possessing a sufficiently disciplined relationship to Jesus. In rural working-class culture, a highly formal kind of discipline often serves as a proof of virtue, a way of contradicting the way the social system of reward distribution seems not to confirm the worth or value of people in that situation in life. By manifesting strict discipline, they contradict the low value they are assigned in the culture and affirm their true capacity and virtue.

Like many rural conservatives, evangelicals tend to order the world into rigid moral categories such as the saved and the damned. Large categories of understanding replace more flexible, detailed, and scientific ways of knowing that are only available to better educated people in, usually, more wealthy regions. Their way of knowing also operates within a narrow range. Conservatives view the world empirically out to an horizon and fear what lies beyond, especially if that takes the form of institutions like the federal government and the United Nations that take income from them in the form of taxes and thus appear to be threats to their ability to survive in a harsh economic world founded on the principle of mutual predation or "competition." For them, the world operates according to rules that seem beyond their knowledge and control. Insufficiently educated and untrained to perform critical thinking, they see the world imperfectly and inaccurately. The way the world works, especially as it affects their lives in terms of prices, taxes, and employment, seems a matter of fatality, and their pessimistic understanding of it, shaped by a sense of frustration or inability to affect its operations in an empowered way, means that the only way it can be "saved" is through some entirely illogical, arational event like the direct intervention of an all-powerful being who can set right the seemingly uncontrollable forces that now trouble their lives. In a sense, Christ in evangelical life is what Hitler was to conservative Germans in the 1930s – an all-powerful savior who compensates for their economic disempowerment. The same emotional matrix explains why such people have in the past been attracted to conservative authoritarian political forms such as Nazism that supply comfort and security, a rigid sense of direction that addresses and rectifies the forces that overwhelm them.

In contemporary America, those overwhelming forces are by and large associated in conservative discourse with liberals and with government. Liberals seek to change the world, to make it a better place, and they do that by taking hard-earned money from rural conservatives who can ill afford to have it taken away. The rules of capitalist economics allocate them scarce resources so that a financially powerful elite minority (many of whom are another, quite different kind of "conservative") can lay claim to much more for itself. The result is religious ideologies such as evangelical Christianity that link liberalism with threats to physical and "spiritual" survival. In *Left Behind*, the villain is someone named Nicolae Carpathia, a European who is associated with liberal causes such as the desire to eliminate hunger and economic inequality and who operates through the United Nations. That in the narrative such things turn out to be the work of the Devil is a metaphor for the fact that liberalism can be harmful to rural conservative constituencies. It erodes traditional assumptions about what is morally permissible that provide a sense of stability in an unstable and uncaring economic world in which failure can result in homelessness and death, and it erodes incomes by taxing for the sake of supporting government programs to alleviate poverty and to spread social justice. Rural conservatives compensate for their victimization by seeking great control over their environments, and authoritarianism provides such a sense of control. Liberals in such a vision are dangerous because they remove control to distant places in Washington, New York, and elsewhere.

Eventually, in the *Left Behind* series the prayer group that will save the world from the liberal Anti-Christ evolves into a paramilitary group, and that narrative evolution registers a geographic reality of rural conservative evangelical culture, which is also steeped in pro-gun ideology. The narrative enacts a structure in their lives that places religion and gun ownership side by side. The forces that threaten rural conservatives consist of economic rules that allocate them very little in regard to material resources and educational capital. Because one aspect of their victimization consists of a failed educational system that does not prepare them to see the world accurately, complexly, and critically, they react to those forces without the help of trained intelligences that are capable of critical analysis, and as a result, they react with violence. The most successful ruse of right-wing ideology in the US consists of directing attention away from the root and real causes of the economic distress that makes the lives of rural conservatives so crimped and painful, and turning it against such things as the United Nations and liberalism, potential solutions to the very economic inequality that is the root cause of the suffering of rural conservatives. The examination of how such ideologies work is important given recent human history, since such ideologies have in the past (Germany in the 1930s, for example) led to highly destructive wars.

Ideology defined as mistaken cognition is common in societies such as the US that are characterized by high levels of economic inequality that must somehow be justified to participants in the society. The US has an extremely high level of inequality, yet people accept it even though they do not benefit. Why is that the case? Scholars of Cultural Studies vary in their approach to this problem. Some argue that Americans are distracted from accurate perception by the endless, ongoing experience of television, driving, and shopping in malls. To watch endless commercials on television is to allow oneself to be subjected to relentless propaganda that distracts one from seeing the wizard behind the curtain, the economic machinery that requires the shaping of minds and perceptions so that people assist, apparently voluntarily, in the construction of the very economic pyramid that is counter to their interests. By continuing to work and buy, we provide the lift that those at the pinnacle of the economic pyramid, the small minority that garners a lot of wealth from all of our combined economic activities, need in order to stay at the top. And by staying at the top, they push everyone else down simply through the "natural," "automatic" operations of the economy.

Others argue that the media shape perceptions so that the society is perceived as being driven by striving individuals rather than social groups that might be said to share a "class" interest, such as corporate executives or bankers or business groups who benefit inordinately more than workers from the way the economy works. Other scholars note that certain ideas that are current in other cultures such as France are not current here. Those ideas concern fairness, equality, distributive justice, and a guarantee of well-being for all. France, where socialist thinking is more pronounced and more common, publicly discusses how to share the wealth all generate between labor and owners. The presence of such ideas is associated with strong labor unions and much greater economic equality. The presence or absence of certain ideas in a culture seems linked to wealth distribution in the economy. Other scholars look at history and note that those in favor of economic inequality successfully marginalized and even suppressed the kinds of egalitarian ideas one finds in France during the period after World War II in the US. Those ideas were branded as being "communist" and were successfully stigmatized. The inegalitarians were able then to mobilize public perceptions in ways favorable to their position that economic inequality is a good thing. No other ideas were in circulation in the media to contradict that assumption and the perception it promoted. "Freedom" prevailed, and that it was indistinguishable from increased levels of inequality went unnoticed.

The ideology of freedom is in many respects a perfect example of how ideas can make things happen in the world when they attach to a successful use of rhetoric to convince people of the virtue of the ideas. In the 1960s and 1970s, Americans were still comfortable with the idea that government had a role to play in economic life, tempering the disparity in wealth distribution by taxing the wealthy and assisting the poor. But a severe economic downturn in the 1970s made it possible for conservatives – who dislike government taxation and regulation of economic activity because it interferes with an over-accumulation of social resources that some wealthy conservatives feel is mandatory for their well-being – to foster discontent with this approach. Other, more poor conservatives see the fruits of their hard work taken from them in taxes that seem unfairly to go to others. Why should their survival be threatened to assure the survival of others who do not seem to work as hard? In situations of economic distress of the sort that emerged in the 1970s, such feelings are perfectly understandable. But the solution is to change the situation that generates distress, not to allow primitive feelings to prevail. That did not happen in the 1970s because conservatives were more successful at mobilizing popular support through such cultural activities as political advertising and movies than liberals. It was easier to promote a happy-feeling word like *freedom* (which meant removing liberal restraints on the over-accumulation of social resources by wealthy conservatives) than a dismal-sounding idea like *government regulation*. When people were feeling hedged in by a bad economic situation, they were more attracted to a slogan or word that seemed to guarantee liberation from constraints.

Conservative Ronald Reagan's television commercials for his presidential campaigns were masterful exercises in visual rhetoric that swayed voters to vote for policies that were dangerous to the world and harmful ultimately to their own economic interests, as everyone finally discovered in 2008, when the "free market" ideology Reagan promoted finally crashed in a display of malfeasance, irresponsibility, and simple greed-motivated skullduggery. Bad thinking wedded to bad motives finally showed what it was capable of. But it would have been difficult to tell from the ads Reagan used that the future held such a disaster.

Consider this ad from 1984: http://www.youtube.com/watch?v=EU-IBF8nwSY.[1] Notice how it uses a very smooth set of editing transitions to communicate a sense of comfort and ease. There are no sharp edits between contrasting images. Just in its technique, it creates a sense of harmony and unity, and it is a very unified White America that is depicted. But is largely the America of the well-to-do, those with jobs and enough money to get married. It is also a highly selective vision that leaves out lots of American life that would have made for some very sharp contrast edits were all of those other dimensions depicted. There are no poor Blacks, for example, or even successful ones, for that matter. Images of Black poverty would have been reminders that it was not "morning in America" for everyone, and the image of successful Blacks would have contradicted the conservative image of Blacks as "welfare cheats" who were incapable of economic success when given a chance. Notice too that all the shots are roughly similar – medium shots of happy events. This creates a sense of a stable reality, one that audiences can take as real and true, one worth preserving and fighting for. The final part of the ad suggests the purpose of this when it refers to American "strength." What that meant at the time was a reassertion of US military power in foreign policy to shore up conservative economic elites around the world and to stop the uprising of poor people against such economic elites. It was class warfare on a world scale, and America under Reagan's leadership was always on the wrong side – promoting and supporting ruthless militaries that massacred civilians or death squads that routinely abused human rights and murdered opponents of wealthy conservative economic oligarchs in countries such as El Salvador and Nicaragua.

During the same period, conservative filmmakers such as Francis Coppola used movies to drive home the Reaganite argument. *Apocalypse*

Now (1979) argues from a conservative perspective that liberals were too weak to conduct foreign policy properly. The threat of enemies abroad (mostly again, poor people's movements for economic justice) required toughness, viciousness, and the will to transcend both legal and human laws and rules in order to defend the right of a small conservative minority to over-accumulate social resources. Later, such arguments would be used to justify the breach of international laws in regard to torture. Those later arguments are already visible in *Apocalypse Now*. The narrative is structured as a struggle between the heroic, conservative individualist and the bureaucratic military establishment that serves as a metaphor for liberalism throughout the film. A CIA assassin is assigned to go into the jungle to find Walter Kurtz, a renegade Special Forces colonel. The assassin is portrayed as a lost soul who is weak and out of control at the start of the narrative. As he pursues his assignment, he realizes that Kurtz is not a renegade; he is in fact a genius who has figured out how to defeat the Communist insurgents in Vietnam by being vicious and by operating outside the rules of war. Along the route of his journal, the assassin sees how ineffective the American military is. In contrast, Kurtz is supremely effective, but to do so, he has had to leave the military establishment behind. In the end, the assassin becomes an initiate of Kurtz and carries out his assignment of assassinating Kurtz with the needed viciousness. He then become Kurtz's replacement with his army of indigenous fighters. The film draws on myths of the Fisher King, whereby an initiate kills the old king in order to replace him, thus fulfilling a cycle of death and rebirth.

Throughout, the indigenous insurgents are portrayed in a racist manner as almost animalistic killers who serve as a model for the conservative argument of the film that one must leave liberal rules behind to succeed. One must compete with viciousness. In one sequence, the regular military attack a village known to be an insurgent headquarters. The sequence depicts schoolchildren who would appear to seem innocent but in fact they conceal insurgent killers who deceive and kill American soldiers. The motif of the treachery of the adversary is common in conservative ideological discourse largely because it is a mirror of conservative thinking itself, which is inclined to be deceptive and to misrepresent reality for the purpose of self-interest. The way this sequence is constructed is a good example of this tendency. Americans are depicted as victims of treachery. A woman runs toward one helicopter and throws a hidden grenade inside, killing a recently wounded soldier. She is then chased down and killed. This sequence inverts actual events such as the US attack on the village of My Lai, where over a hundred civilians were murdered by American soldiers. In the film, in a move common to conservative thinking, one's own bad motives are assigned to the adversary to justify one's own bad motives for violating their rights.

The primary character, Walter Kurtz, a renegade Special Forces colonel who "goes it alone" against the enemy, defying his superiors and achieving spectacular results by using the enemy's hit-and-run tactics, is constructed as a repository of conservative values of the kind that would in American society justify deregulating financial markets especially so that private gain would trump the good of the community as that is embodied in government. The film argues that such individualism is superior to "bureaucratic" institutions that are ineffective in fighting the enemy. *Bureaucracy* was a word conservatives used to characterize liberal governance in the 1970s and 1980s. In the world, liberal regulatory government was portrayed as restraining heroic economic entrepreneurs who, according to conservatives, would save America from the economic recession of the 1970s, which according to this argument, was caused by excessively costly government regulation of business. In the film, bureaucracy takes the form of government outposts that have no leader, rules of war that hamper effective action, less-than-serious military commanders, soldiers distracted by entertainment instead of becoming hardened killers like the enemy, and misguided policies that hamper the truly effective individualist. Just as political conservatives argued that heroic individualist entrepreneurs operating without any communal restraints or government regulations would save America financially and economically, the film argues that the Vietnam War would have been won if heroic individualists who possess superior intuition and a willingness to operate outside community rules were left free to pursue the war in their own way. Conservatives would come to endorse the murder of adversaries without due process through surrogate death squads in the 1980s and to endorse torture, a crime against humanity, in the later war against terrorism, and in the film, almost in preparation for these events, Kurtz summarily executes suspected spies without trial. The film notes that after he did this, enemy activity decreased markedly, thus endorsing his breach of human and legal rules. That such extralegal activity serves as a metaphor in the film for the conservative economic ideal of unregulated entrepreneurship would be one of the ironies of the global economic collapse brought on by conservative economic theory in action in 2008.

Student Exercise

In American culture, you will find many examples of the ideology of freedom. View *Fight Club* and examine it from the point of view of ideology. How is the film ideological? What personal ideal does it foster? And how is that ideal linked to the kind of violent resentment directed against liberals that one finds in right-wing evangelical culture? Are there other similarities to the *Left Behind* series or with *Apocalypse Now*?

Note

1. "Ronald Reagan TV Ad: 'It's Morning in America Again,'" http://www.youtube.com/watch?v=EU-IBF8nwSY (accessed October 8, 2009).

Sources

For a general introduction, see James Decker, *Ideology* (Houndsmills, UK, 2004); and David Hawkes, *Ideology* (New York, 2003). On the connection between ideology and self-identity, see Louis Althusser, "Ideology and Ideological State Apparatuses" in Louis Althusser, *Lenin and Philosophy* (London, 1971); and Gordon Bailey, *Ideology: Structuring Identities in Contemporary Life* (Peterborough, UK, 2003). On ideology considered as a system of ideas, see J. Schwarzmantel, *Ideology and Politics* (Thousand Oaks, Calif., 2008); and Robert Porter, *Ideology: Contemporary Social, Political, and Cultural Theory* (Cardiff, 2006). On ideology defined as a form of consciousness, see Patricia Ewick, ed., *Consciousness and Ideology* (Burlington, Vt., 2006); and Ron Eyerman, *False Consciousness and Ideology in Marxist Theory* (Stockholm, 1981).

5

Rhetoric

with Brett Ingram

Rhetoric has a bad reputation. Often used as an insult in the contemporary political scene, the word *rhetoric* has come to suggest mere verbal trickery set in contrast to real action, the ornamental play of words rather than serious and responsible attention to facts. For instance, it is a common strategy for one political candidate to frame his or her opponent as a dealer in fanciful rhetoric while positioning himself or herself as a "straight talker," more "down to earth," and therefore more authentic and capable of enacting change. Examples of this strategy abounded in the 2008 US presidential campaign, as Republican candidate John McCain and Democratic hopeful Hillary Clinton both attempted to halt the momentum of Barack Obama by calling into the question the substance behind Obama's eloquent speaking style. John McCain cautioned voters to "listen carefully, because his ideas are not always as impressive as his rhetoric."[1] Likewise, Hillary Clinton stated, "Some people may think words are change. You and I know better. Words are cheap."[2] Bill Clinton, himself an acknowledged master of wordplay, added, "I think that action counts more than rhetoric, that solutions are more important than speeches, however beautiful."[3] We can see here a dichotomy being constructed, in which ideas and action are set in opposition to linguistic expression; the former are represented as forces capable of making thing happen, while the latter is rendered as naïve idealism, pleasing to the ear but ultimately ineffectual as a means of transforming the real world.

What must be noted is that the Clintons' and McCain's attacks are themselves rhetorical, that is, they are intentionally composed arrangements of language designed to provide an interpretive framework through which the listener is prompted to think and act in a prescribed way. These rhetorical constructions are formulated not simply to provide a fleeting stimulation to the listener's senses and emotions, but also to actually move bodies and resources – in this case, the bodies of voters into voting booths, and of political power to one candidate rather than another. While we may not often think of words as having the same force as actions or objects – recall the well-worn adage "Sticks and stones may break my bones but words can never hurt me" – the fact is that words have tremendous power. Words are what we use to motivate people to action.

Rhetoric is the strategic use of language in the effort to induce others to respond to our needs and desires. This need not be understood as a sinister enterprise; indeed, it is a necessary, even inescapable part of the human condition. We are all rhetoricians. Many theorists of rhetoric would argue that a statement as seemingly innocuous as "Please pass the salt" is a rhetorical act in which a speaker imposes her will upon the world. The speaker has identified an internal need (more flavor in her food), strategically chosen to begin her sentence with a word that will create a context of goodwill and therefore increase the likelihood of her request being granted ("please"), designated the physical action she wishes her interlocutor to perform ("pass"), and pinpointed the object of her desire in space ("the salt"). This same speaker, upon finishing her dinner, may employ similar strategies to persuade her friends that it is a better idea to watch *The Simpsons* rather than *American Idol*, to organize a search party for a missing toddler, or to convince a crowd that the right to club baby seals must be protected by the US Constitution. Whatever the ethical dimensions of the cause, rhetoric is, simply put, the way people get things done. While politicians and other professional rhetoricians may disparage rhetoric as unscrupulous, cynically manipulative, and something that the *other* guy does, the fact is that every use of language that is directed toward others for the purpose of compelling action is rhetorical in nature.

We may at first recoil from the idea that our words are intended to make people do things for us, and argue that we are simply telling the truth about what we are thinking. However, here we must pause and reflect upon what it means to "tell the truth." Many contemporary theorists in the humanities and social sciences agree that what individuals believe to be true is arrived at through an ongoing process of negotiation and persuasion that occurs at every level of cultural life, from interpersonal relationships to social institutions such as government, religion, mass media, and education. At each level of social organization there is a claim to a version of truth which may or may not agree with the truth claims occurring at other levels. In some cultures and contexts, scientists are deemed to have the strongest claim to truth; in others, religious leaders have a stranglehold on the concept. The only truth is that "truth" is constructed by a series of arguments carved from the material of language, not by access to a granite-like reality that is the source of objective, universally agreed-upon certainty.

Think of it this way: even as they physically inhabit the same earth, people everywhere experience different lived realities, and those realities are often in conflict with each other. We can see and hear the same thing, but we often come to very different understandings of what's right there before our eyes. How we make sense of an event is determined by the language we use to describe it to ourselves and to others. The words we choose provide a frame through which we comprehend reality, the same way a camera frame focuses your attention on some aspects of a scene while blocking out others. When you take a picture of something, you must make a judgment as to what is most important in the scene that you wish to capture, and what can be cut out. When later you show someone the picture you have taken, they will only see what you've decided you want them to see, and will interpret the event you photographed accordingly. Rhetoric works the same way. Consider the difference between describing a foreign-born person who is living in the US without the government's knowledge as an *illegal alien* or as an *undocumented worker*. The former designation immediately casts the person into the same "criminal" category as thieves and murderers, with all the frightening emotions this brings with it, while the word *alien* brings to mind the most extreme and unknowable form of difference, embodied in the popular imagination by the creature from outer space. The subconscious associations it inspires are those of danger and threat. On the other hand, *undocumented worker* positively highlights the person's labor and productivity, and implies that it is simply a matter of bureaucratic red tape and some paperwork that separates the person from being just like any other American citizen. Both *illegal alien* and *undocumented worker* are technically "true" descriptions of the type of person in question, but the selection of one rhetorical frame rather than the other will determine which truth is accepted and which is rejected, and will have serious consequences in terms of how people feel about and act toward individuals bearing this status.

Those who wish to crack down on "illegals" and those who think such terminology is unfair can both make claims to evidence which will back up their arguments. The former can point to the legal codes which make residency without government approval unlawful, and the latter can claim that these codes have always been subject to revision as historical circumstances change. But rhetoric has the ability to sway people even when it is not reinforced by evidence of any kind; in fact, it is often most potent when it cannot be traced back to an original source. We've probably all been subject to hurtful rumors at some point in our lives, and therefore know that what makes them so maddening is that once they are in circulation, they take on a life of their own and can become nearly impossible to disprove by rational means. Rationality is irrelevant when people find it more titillating or interesting to blindly believe something is true rather than to painstakingly search for reasonable evidence to support or negate the claim. Institutions which have an investment in securing people's attention and assent, such as political parties and media corporations, know this, and disseminate rumors as a rhetorical method for altering the public discourse. For instance, in the 2000 Republican presidential primary campaign, many voters in South Carolina found anonymous leaflets under their windshield wipers that "revealed" Senator John McCain had fathered an illegitimate child with an African American woman (in actuality, he had adopted a child from Mother Theresa's orphanage in Bangladesh). Drawing as it did on deep-seated racial prejudices still lingering in the Deep South, the rumor proved more scandalously enthralling and therefore more believable than fact. McCain lost the South Carolina primary, and the presidential nomination, to George W. Bush. With the emergence of the Internet as a channel of information available to most Americans, rumor spreading has become even more efficient. In the 2008 presidential election, a false rumor that Senator Barack Obama was a Muslim appeared in millions of e-mail inboxes, and according to polls, successfully convinced 13 percent of Americans of its veracity, many of whom cited Obama's religious affiliation as a reason they did not vote for him in the primary election (although despite this, he did manage to gain his party's nomination).

What makes this case unique is that Obama chose to combat the rumor by using his enemies' medium against them: his campaign built a website that offered refutations to the rumors, and encouraged visitors to the site to upload their online address books and send viral e-mails – essentially "truth rumors" – to their friends. Obama recognized that information technology has changed the way people experience public discourse. Before the Internet and cable news boom of the 1990s, it was considered easier to divide information sources according to expectations of reliability and trustworthiness: tabloid shows and newspapers provided sensational entertainment, while the news broadcasts of the major networks aspired toward objective and unbiased reportage. But these boundaries are becoming increasingly blurred as news channels try to spice up their programming by giving voice to the most extreme positions, and by devoting much of their airtime to tawdry stories that generate high ratings rather than to serious, thoughtful political debate and analysis. At the same time, the Web introduced millions of new rhetorics into public discourse, each with its own claim to "true" knowledge. Given this cacophony of discordant world-views, it has become almost impossible to distill fact from fiction. More than ever, it is widely accepted that truth is in the eye of the beholder, and that rather than seeking to form some public consensus about truth, at best we can take into account multiple interpretations of the same reality, and decide for ourselves which one we choose to believe.

Most people are fairly certain that they can figure out what is true and what is false, and they often become angry at others who disagree with their calculations, accusing them of willfully distorting "the facts" through the cynical use of rhetoric in order to deceive and manipulate. However, because there is no final word on what counts as "truth," it is very difficult to satisfactorily settle these arguments. Consequently, rhetoric is often considered to be synonymous with lying.

The debasement of rhetoric is nothing new; in fact, disputes about the wisdom, ethics, and effectiveness of rhetoric have echoed throughout the institutions of public life since classical times. Plato, in making his case against the Sophists – teachers of rhetoric in fifth-century BC Athens who promised to turn their students into persuasive and influential public speakers … for a hefty price – famously denounced rhetoric as "mere cookery," suggesting that rhetoric is to the soul what delicious but unhealthy foods are to the body: it gives the temporary illusion of well-being, but ultimately corrupts the individual who falls prey to its temptations. Plato argued that rhetoric misleads men from the path to true knowledge and virtue. The Sophists, on the other hand, did not believe there was such a thing as true knowledge and virtue. Instead, they held that, in the words of the Sophist Protagoras, "man is the measure of all things." In other words, lacking a practically accessible supernatural judge of truth, justice, and virtue, humans are left to determine the meanings of these ideas amongst themselves, using persuasive arguments crafted in language and addressed to the public. The processes by which humans seek to attain truth or certainty – philosophical reasoning, prayer, and the scientific method – are socially constructed rather than naturally given. According to the Sophists, there is nothing irrational, immoral, or unnatural about pointing out that we can make things happen using language, for our ideas about reason, morals, and nature are themselves the products of human language use. Philosophers, religious leaders, and scientists constantly revise and reinterpret their ideas based on arguments that take place within their professional circles. They all work to convince each other that their way is the "correct" way, and that a particular course of action is preferable to another. A Sophist would claim they are all simply rhetoricians in denial.

Protagoras' dictum is often interpreted negatively as a statement of radical moral relativism and individual self-interest – if there is no logic or order underpinning the moral laws that govern society, then it follows that anything is permissible, and anarchy is inevitable. However, this reading of Protagoras is founded on a very pessimistic understanding of human nature. It assumes humans are inherently unruly, selfish, and in servitude to their primal passions, and thus require a powerful central authority to keep them in line and provide moral guidance and rules. A more generous understanding of Protagoras' statement would interpret it as a declaration of independence from oppressive superstition, and of confidence in people's ability to cultivate human culture and civilization as a corrective to barbarism and animality. Far from licensing everyone to indulge in appalling behavior, the statement could suggest that the individual must attend to the community in order to cooperatively construct a mutually beneficial means of survival in nature. In order to form these communal bonds, there must be some shared meaning, something on which people can at least cautiously and imperfectly agree, and there must be some human intentionality behind the selection and advocacy of one meaning rather than another. In other words, there must be rhetoric. Rhetoric is the way people organize the chaos of experience into cohesive, shared world-views through persuasive public discourse. Without rhetoric, there could be no society. Of course, people have a pervasive and tragic habit of using rhetoric to build value systems founded on principles of exclusivity and exploitation, but by the same token, rhetoric can be used to critique and reform inhumane social institutions and cultural practices. Indeed, rhetoric's strength as a critical tool is not in its methodological usefulness for establishing a stable sense of what *is*, but rather, its adaptability to changing social conditions and its practical use value as an instrument for setting into action the forces that determine what *should* be, and what *can* be.

While rhetoric was considered a vitally important element in the development and maintenance of human societies in the ancient world, its centrality in the study of contemporary culture was not established until relatively recently. From the 1920s through the 1960s, rhetorical studies was primarily understood as a discipline tied to the teaching of public speaking, and its focus tended to be on the analysis of speeches removed from their cultural and historical contexts. This changed in the 1970s and 1980s, due in large part to the emergence of television as a primary medium of public discourse, the rise of grassroots political movements that represented the marginalized and the oppressed, and the influence of European philosophers such as Mikhail Bakhtin, Michel Foucault, Jacques Derrida, and Paul de Man. This led a new generation of American rhetorical theorists such as Lloyd Bitzer, Edwin Black, Wayne Booth, Michael McGee, and Raymond McKerrow to start rethinking, among other things, the possibility or desirability of objective knowledge, the monolithic concept of the "the audience," and the relation between language use and political power. These scholars were among the first to work at the intersection of rhetorical theory and cultural criticism, and to conceive of rhetoric theory as a valuable resource in the struggle for progressive social change.

Kenneth Burke was massively influential to the new rhetorical theorists. A fundamental Burkean contribution to rhetorical studies was the move away from the traditional association of rhetoric with acts of *persuasion*, and toward the more elaborate idea of rhetoric as the process of *identification*, which is rooted in the notion of *substance*. According to Burke, we form our sense of selves by our identifications with various symbolic entities, which may include job titles, leisure activities, religious affiliations, nationalities, and value systems. All of these symbols are in some respects abstract ideas, yet they have a power to move bodies that is as real as air or water, and must be understood to be equally substantial. As we identify with these things, we become *consubstantial* with them – we share the same substance. So, for instance, to be "American" is, in one sense, merely to mentally associate with an idea that has no material foundation – there is no physical property that makes one literally American the way that a certain genetic coding makes one human (of course, it can be argued that even the connection between a genetic sequence and "humanness" is a rhetorical construct with no ultimate basis in truth). However, once you have identified with the symbolic concept of "American," you are compelled, consciously and unconsciously, to act in specific, physical ways. You may feel an adrenaline rush of anger as you watch footage of elected officials betraying the public trust, or experience a flush of warmth when the national anthem plays before a baseball game. You may be obligated to kill or be killed in war, or be confined to a cell because you transgressed American codes of acceptable behavior. Identifications have very real material, bodily effects; in identifying with these symbols, we become consubstantial with other people who have made the same identification.

Burke proposed that "you persuade a man only insofar as you talk his language by speech, gesture, tonality, order, image, attitude, idea, *identifying* your ways with his."[4] Burke widens the reach of rhetoric to encompass not only public speech but also meaningful performative acts (that is, speech acts that make things happen in the world such as "seal a deal") which are directed toward persuasion and identification. These may include physical gestures, clothing, the layout of museum exhibits or public memorials, the interior design of workplaces or classrooms … anything that seeks to manage the way an experience is interpreted and understood. Burke claims, "Wherever there is persuasion, there is rhetoric. And wherever there is 'meaning,' there is 'persuasion.'"[5] A presidential candidate's decision to address her audience as "my fellow Americans," the flag pin she prominently wears on her lapel, and the patriotic music that accompanies her walk to the podium are all instances of rhetoric, insofar as they are intended to convince the audience that the candidate has something in common with them, and that she is thus positioned to act in their best interests, for these are her interests as well. Burke does not eliminate persuasion from his definition of rhetoric, but rather incorporates it into the larger process by which people come to change their attitudes and actions. For Burke, persuasion, identification, and consubstantiality are not three distinct phenomena, but terms that imply each other: no act of persuasion can occur unless the rhetorician can find a common substance with which he and his interlocutors can both identify. Once this identification is established, the rhetorician and the audience are consubstantial with each other through their shared interests, or at least the impression of shared interests that has been created through the rhetorician's skillful deployment of symbols.

Yet no matter how united people are in their identifications, they still remain fundamentally distinct beings. People obviously do not literally fuse together into one physical body, and each individual identifies himself with many different substances. A man may consider himself to be a proud American, and yet still vehemently oppose the policies of the American government. The meaning of "American" is unstable – to some people it implies loyalty to a political party, to others it suggests belief in certain values that exist independently of political parties, and to still others it might merely be a geographical designation. As a site of conflicting interpretations, it is a symbol that invites both cohesion and division. Any substance contains the potential for division; as Burke says, "If men were not apart from one another, there would be no need for the rhetorician to proclaim their unity."[6] In other words, if we were truly of one substance – if everyone in the world absolutely agreed upon the meaning of every symbol and the wisdom of every judgment – an ideal state of universal harmony would exist, and articulating our shared interests would be redundant and unnecessary. However, we know this is not the case. In reality, identification comes with its counterpart, division. To say "I am *this*," usually implies, "Because I am not *that*." People have a tendency to draw the boundaries of a social group and promote group cohesion by targeting and screening out those who do not "properly" belong to it. The excluded "others" are then rhetorically framed as a threat to the social order. Thus defined, the banished group is forced to bear the weight of blame for problems that arise in the community, and their persecution is made to seem justifiable. Burke points out, "Men who can unite on nothing else can unite on the basis of a foe shared by all."[7] Rhetoric is capable of fostering collective action, but this cooperative spirit often comes with a heavy price.

For example, it is easy enough to claim that we are Americans because we support life, liberty, and the pursuit of happiness, and that those who do not value such qualities are un-American. Things become decidedly more muddled when we're called upon to define what exactly we mean by *life, liberty, pursuit,* and *happiness*. To what authority can we refer to assure other cultures that we have dominion over the "correct" meanings of these terms? And furthermore, can those people who identify themselves as Americans even agree amongst themselves as to the correct interpretations? In trying to disentangle ourselves from such quandaries, we again find ourselves caught in a web of language from which there is no escape except through the production of more language.

Such a state of high-stakes ambiguity is, in Burke's words, an "invitation to rhetoric," as different groups scramble to devise and disseminate comprehensive interpretive frameworks – or "ideologies" – that support understandings of the world which are conducive to their particular interests.[8] We are implicated together by our reliance on the resources of the world, and also separated from each other by our status as distinct physical bodies each with its own set of needs and desires. We draw upon rhetoric as a means of negotiating the simultaneous and contradictory conditions of interdependence and alienation that are inherent to human experience. Rhetoric intersects with power when ideologies founded on the exploitation of particular social groups and the unequal distribution of limited resources are expressed, justified, and maintained through everyday language and public discourse.

As academic disciplines in the humanities and social sciences turn their attention toward public discourse and take what is often referred to as the *interpretive turn* – the awareness that the beliefs and practices that structure any form of human activity are socially constructed and inevitably serve the political interests of one group rather than another – the concerns of rhetorical studies and cultural studies increasingly intersect. Both are invested in issues of power, performance, popular discourse, textuality, and interpretation and concerned with the ways people struggle for agency within economic and political structures using symbolic resources such as everyday language and artistic expression.

Fight Club is an example of a text that is concerned with the role rhetoric plays in contemporary society. It portrays the conflicted conscience, and consciousness, of a man who has achieved material success in the corporate world, yet finds himself tormented by a feeling of emptiness when the consumer goods he has acquired fail to provide him with a sense of meaning and purpose. Indeed, the protagonist not only lacks a spiritual sense of self, but also literally has no identity except that which is provided by cultural products: he refers to himself only as "Jack," a name he sardonically borrows from a series of mass market self-help books he finds moldering in the basement of an abandoned house. The message is clear to the spectator: we have no intrinsic, "true" selves, but rather, we are formed by the texts we consume. In a capitalist society like America, the rhetorical purpose of those texts is often to convince us we are lacking something (e.g., physical attractiveness, ideal health, social respectability, or sexual organs of reasonable size or shape), and then to persuade us that buying a certain item will fill that lack. To illustrate this, in one scene we see prices materialize onscreen as Jack moves through his apartment. In a voiceover, he tells us that he'd flip through catalogs and ask, "What kind of dining set defines me as a person?" Jack has been persuaded by the rhetoric of advertising, and hopes to in turn create rhetorical "advertisements for himself" using the things he owns. The film encourages us to question: are there no such things as truth, virtue, or beauty that transcend the cynical world of consumer capitalism? Is our worth as human beings equivalent to our worth in material assets? We hear echoes of Plato's lament to the Sophists, who were, you'll recall, the slick marketers of their day, promising to increase the social status of their clients in exchange for money.

Jack's existential torment is alleviated when he encounters Tyler Durden, a charismatic anarchist who counsels him to cast away his earthly possessions, and to seek spiritual clarity and redemption through subversive action rather than obsessive self-reflection. Tyler is presented as an ironic Christ figure, a latter-day prophet who preaches the gospel of principled non-conformity and anti-materialism (and, of course, casual, consensual violence). The film makes a persuasive case for Tyler's ideology, only to later, arguably, undercut it. Disenchanted by the rhetoric of capitalism, which prompts consumers to identify with abstract entities like brand logos rather than with real human beings, Jack is seduced by Tyler's counter-rhetoric, which takes the notion of human contact, so missing in Jack's life, to its literal extreme: the men of *Fight Club* forge meaningful relationships through their exchange of blows and the intermingling of their blood. They seem to attain what Kenneth Burke calls *consubstantiality*, a new kind of self-identity through the group or community.[9]

Fight Club makes its rhetorical appeal through its use of visual devices and dialogue. The fight scenes, which are shot in warm colors and feature glistening flesh and intimate physicality, are portrayed with a lush sensuality, even an eroticism, which stands in marked contrast to the bleak sterility and drab tones of scenes depicting office life. Tyler's words are smart, funny, and romantic; set against the dull discourse of the workplace, they take on added resonance. The spectator may find it difficult not to be swayed by Tyler's argument, which is essentially a diatribe against rhetoric: Tyler frames consumer capitalism as an exercise in manipulation and domination that hides behind pretty words and images. As a substitute, he espouses a value system that privileges free-thinking individualism and the "honesty" of violence stripped of the ideological pretensions – such as patriotism or heroism – in which mainstream society often cloaks it. Tyler elevates action over words, and "true knowledge" of human nature over the rhetorically constructed conventions of social propriety. The film aspires to step outside discourse and language altogether, into a realm of pure nature, stripped bare, like the men's bodies.

The underground fighting communities begin to change as they spread across the country. What began as a project based on anti-authoritarianism and non-conformity becomes something that resembles the regimentation and uniformity of the corporate world from which Jack sought escape. In his professional life, Jack was compelled to wear a suit and tie, and to function as a nameless cog in the capitalist machine. *Fight Club* initially offered an alternative: it allowed him and the other participants to test their strength and resolve in an arena far removed from the impersonal trappings of consumer culture. But consider what happens when "recruits" start to show up at Jack and Tyler's door seeking membership in what has become something of a guerilla army. They acquire identities through naming; rhetoric would seem to be inevitably a part of even this most "natural" of groups that supposedly found a way out of the artifice of civilization. To be a group, it must engage in acts of identification through discourse and become "Space Monkeys." Old names for new, and not true nature for false nurture.

Ultimately, we learn that Tyler is merely an hallucination, and that Jack alone led the Space Monkeys to plan and execute "Project Mayhem," a plot to blow up the headquarters of financial corporations and erase everyone's debt. We know that Jack is not a physically imposing man, and yet he has successfully organized a massive effort to destroy the institutions of financial capitalism, a testament to the power of rhetoric to move minds and bodies. In the memorable and ambiguous final shot of *Fight Club*, we see Jack and Marla holding hands as the skyscrapers explode and fall around them. It is unclear whether we are supposed to read this as a good thing or a bad thing. Is it a criminal act of terrorism, or a revolutionary gesture of emancipation? On what moral or ethical criteria do you base your judgment? On what foundations of "truth" do you rely in making your decision? How might you use rhetoric to convince others that your interpretation of the film's conclusion is "correct"?

In September 2008, Republican Senator John McCain faced a daunting challenge in the presidential race. Polls indicated that he trailed Democratic Senator Barack Obama by a significant margin, and furthermore, momentum seemed to be on Obama's side. Weary of the belligerent foreign policies and ethical scandals that characterized the conservative Bush administration, the United States seemed ready for dramatic change in leadership, and the idealistic, progressive Obama represented a radical departure. McCain, on the other hand, was closely associated with Bush's conservative, traditional vision of America, in terms of both his politics and his appearance; as we know, the rhetorical effect of visual signs must be taken seriously, and the youthful, multiracial Obama stood in stark relief against the elderly, White McCain. In order to reinvigorate his campaign, McCain chose a running mate that took the public and the press by surprise: Sarah Palin, a young Alaskan governor with very little political experience, virtually no exposure in the national media, and an ideological stance that was even more conservative than McCain's own. Indeed, it initially seemed as if all she had going for her was her gender and her age, for these would both counter Obama's perceived strengths as a candidate who could shatter cultural barriers and bring fresh new ideas to the office. In her nomination acceptance speech at the Republican National Convention, Palin needed to reframe concerns about her lack of adequate qualifications, renew American's trust in the Republican Party, and redirect public discourse about Barack Obama in order to diminish his reputation and thwart his momentum. By almost all accounts, she was, at least briefly, successful in her efforts: her speech was lavishly praised in the news media, and the McCain-Palin ticket drew even with Obama-Biden in the polls released days after the convention. Using rhetorical analysis, we can examine her speech to uncover the strategies she employed to accomplish her goals.

America prides itself on its egalitarianism, the belief that all Americans are created equal, and that through hard work and self-discipline, any citizen has the opportunity to overcome obstacles of race, class, and gender and achieve "success," which is often associated with wealth, fame, and power. We can see this core myth reinforced through popular American stories from *Mr. Smith Goes to Washington* to *Rocky* to *Forrest Gump* to *Legally Blonde*, all variations on the rags-to-riches theme. Of course, we know that in practical terms, the body and circumstances into which individuals are born stack the deck in favor of some people at the expense of others. However, we also know that people's expectations and attitudes are shaped by the discourses circulating through the culture, and an appealing illusion can often be more believable than the harsh complexities of material reality. Political speeches, like movies, draw upon our dreams and aspirations in order to manufacture a representation or image of the world that is more compelling than everyday life. Lived experience provides the raw material to be artfully refashioned by the speaker into a new version of reality that listeners will want to bring into being through cooperative action.

Palin wanted to erase the popular conception of John McCain as the business-as-usual Washington insider and Barack Obama as the visionary outsider, and script a new narrative in which she stood out as the upstart maverick and McCain emerged as an uncompromising reformer. To do so, Palin makes frequent appeals to the rags-to-riches, common (wo)man versus the establishment mythology so cherished in American culture. Notice how she calls out the "experts in Washington" and the "pollsters and pundits" in her first few paragraphs, and sets up a dichotomy between these figures and McCain. To exhibit expertise is usually considered a positive attribute, especially in a field such as politics that demands a great deal of knowledge, but Palin appears to recast this as a liability. She argues that voters "knew better" than to listen to the experts, pollsters, and pundits.[10] Why might Palin try to establish a tone of hostility toward intellectuals? In rhetorical terms, what is she hoping to accomplish by framing the issue in this way? With whom is the listener encouraged to identify?

Palin very quickly moves into an account of her personal history. We may think it common sense that a candidate for a job that will place her a heartbeat away from the presidency would want to highlight her professional credentials and achievements, yet Palin decides to instead tell us about her humble small-town roots, her family life, and her husband. Why might she share such intimate details in a speech of such tremendous importance? What role does gender play in determining the emphasis of her remarks? Would this same strategy be effective if she was a man? How does she communicate her social class affiliation without making explicit reference to financial wealth? How does Palin's rhetorical framing of gender and class intersect with a conservative value system?

Palin seems to successfully reframe her limited political experience as an asset rather than a liability. Notice how she glorifies her former duties as a PTA mom, a city council representative, and a small-town mayor, and devalues Obama's background as a community organizer in Chicago. In Burkean terms, how is she exploiting rhetoric's capacity to promote identification through consubstantiality? With whom does she encourage the listener to identify, who are cast as "others," and why? How might these selections function within her larger political strategy?

Another problem the Republican Party had to contend with in the election was the public's association of conservatism with Big Business. And for good reason: under the Bush administration, large corporations received massive tax cuts and virtually unfettered access to the wealth made available by the Iraq War. The relationship between corporations and the administration was so cozy that in some instances corporate lobbyists were literally writing government policy. This did not sit well with many Americans, and the electorate seemed eager to rid Washington of corporate interests. McCain, however, supported Bush's tax cuts and wished to make them permanent. As a matter of ideological principle, McCain believed in "small government," the idea that the government should play as little role as possible in the lives of citizens and economic institutions.

One aspect of this belief – lowering taxes – is consistently popular with voters; other aspects – cutting funding to programs such as education and environmental protection, and loosening regulations that keep corporate power in check – tend to be viewed less favorably. Palin sought to downplay the reduction of social services, and foreground the benefits of transferring economic power from the public sector to private interests. Pay attention to the way she rhetorically links tax cuts, the expansion of corporate freedom, and the loosening of environmental protection to post-9/11 fears of terrorism and Islam. Also, note her use of personal anecdote to "shrink" big, complicated issues such as the structure of the economy into a narrative that garners an emotional, rather than an intellectual, response from the listener.[11] It is a common rhetorical tactic, used by progressives and conservatives alike. Do you believe it is an ethical practice? How do you think Plato and Protagoras would answer this question?

Throughout Palin's speech, we find many explicit references to rhetoric. She mentions "the cloud of rhetoric" Obama produces in "dramatic speeches before devoted followers," and the "idealism of high-flown speechmaking, in which crowds are stirringly summoned to support great things." This is set against the "idealism of those leaders, like John McCain, who actually do great things." She says Obama is "a gifted speaker" who can "inspire with his words." In contrast, Palin claims that "John McCain has inspired with his deeds."[12] Though we may find it ironic that Palin delivers these lines in an idealistic speech before a crowd of devoted followers, it should not come as a surprise. Rhetoric is not a practice tied to the political left or right, or even to politicians in general. It is general in our lives. Note as well that her argument is not that different from that in *Fight Club*, a film that also associates liberals with empty speechifying or "rhetoric." The alternative in the film is not that different from the one Palin proposes – an ideal of pure action without much critical or intellectual reflection of the sort educated liberals engage in. Many noted as the Palin campaign unfolded that she appealed to the worst racist instincts of many poor undereducated constituencies, people who do not understand the world very well and are thus easy prey for the extreme right, which appeals to emotion much more than reason and mobilizes resentment against "foreigners" to assuage the pain of economic deprivation. That deprivation often takes the form of debt, of course, and that is the target of *Fight Club*. The overlap between the Palin campaign and the film is most striking, however, in the history that lies behind right-wing appeals to the poor and undereducated. When those appeals were most successful, in

Germany in the 1920s and 1930s, for example, they resulted in the actual formation of "fight clubs," boxing organizations made up largely of disgruntled World War I veterans who felt betrayed by German liberals and who rose up against them in the Nazi movement.

Student Exercise

Find a use of rhetoric in the world around you and examine how it works. You might use the Internet to look up the transcript of Obama's speech to the Democratic National Convention. Does he use rhetorical devices similar to those employed by Palin to create identifications with his audience and motivate them to action? How do the ideological beliefs of Obama and his audience determine the rhetorical frames he employs in his speech?

Or you might choose a current issue that is meaningful to you and study the way it is addressed differently on Fox News and MSNBC. Each of these networks is reputed to carry an ideological bias into its coverage of the news; Fox tends to take a conservative position, and MSNBC often favors a progressive worldview. This will be most evident in the political talk shows both networks feature in their prime time programming. Pay close attention to the language the hosts use to frame the issue, the visual images that accompany the discussion, and the political affiliations of the guest commentators invited on the shows. All of these elements are the result of conscious decisions made by producers, and work together to build an ideological argument. While both networks are technically reporting on the same reality, you'll probably notice that they take very different approaches to describing and interpreting that reality. Your task is to critically analyze what is being implied by the words you hear and symbols you see on the screen. You may then decide to use rhetorical strategies to formulate an argument of your own: which broadcast do you think people should watch? Do you think one channel has a better grasp of the "truth" than the other? How would you use rhetoric to persuade a particular audience that your recommendations should acted upon?

Notes

1. "McCain Criticizes Obama's Educational Policies," MSNBC.com, August 1, 2008, http://www.msnbc.msn.com/id/25968617/ (accessed October 8, 2009).
2. "*Meet the Press* Transcript for Feb. 17, 2008," MSNBC.com, February 17, 2008, http://www.msnbc.msn.com/id/23209237/ (accessed October 8, 2009).
3. "Big Crowd Hears Former President Clinton Campaign for Hillary," Chippewa. com, February 15, 2008, http://www.chippewa.com/articles/2008/02/15/news/ 755d.txt (accessed October 8, 2009).
4. Kenneth Burke, *A Rhetoric of Motives* (Berkeley: University of California Press, 1969), 55.
5. Burke, *A Rhetoric of Motives*, 172.
6. Ibid., 22.
7. Kenneth Burke, "The Rhetoric of Hitler's 'Battle,'" in Kenneth Burke, *The Philosophy of Literary Form: Studies in Symbolic Action* (Berkeley: University of California Press, 1974).
8. See Burke, *A Rhetoric of Motives*.
9. See ibid.
10. "Vice Presidential Candidate Gov. Sarah Palin (AK) Full Speech at the RNC," http://www.youtube.com/watch?v=UCDxXJSucF4 (accessed October 8, 2009).
11. "Vice Presidential Candidate."
12. Ibid.

Sources

See Kenneth Burke, *A Grammar of Motives* (Berkeley, Calif., 1969); Craig Smith, *Rhetoric and Human Consciousness* (Prospect Heights, Ill., 2009); Michael Carrithers, *Culture, Rhetoric, and the Vicissitudes of Life* (New York, 2009); Jennifer Richards, *Rhetoric* (London, 2008); and Barbara Johnstone and Christopher Eisenhart, eds., *Rhetoric in Detail: Discourse Analyses of Rhetorical Talk and Text* (Philadelphia, 2008).

Burke, Kenneth. *A Rhetoric of Motives*. Berkeley: University of California Press, 1969.
Burke, Kenneth. *The Philosophy of Literary Form: Studies in Symbolic Action*. Berkeley: University of California Press, 1974.
Lucaites, John Louis, Celeste Michelle Condit, and Sally Caudill. *Contemporary Rhetorical Theory*. New York: Guilford Press, 1999.

McGee, Michael Calvin. "A Materialist's Conception of Rhetoric." In *Explorations in Rhetoric: Studies in Honor of Douglas Ehninger*, ed. Ray E. McKerrow. Glenview, IL: Scott, Foresman, 1982.

Olson, Lester C., Cara A. Finnegan, and Diane S. Hope, eds. *Visual Rhetoric: A Reader in Communication and American Culture*. Thousand Oaks, CA: 2008.

Plato. *Gorgias*. Oxford: Oxford University Press, 1998.

Rosteck, Thomas, ed. *At the Intersection: Rhetorical Studies and Cultural Studies*. New York: Guilford Press, 1998.

Scott, Robert L. "On Viewing Rhetoric as Epistemic." *Central States Speech Journal* 18 (1967): 9–17.

Selzer, Jack, and Sharon Crowley, eds. *Rhetorical Bodies*. Madison: University of Wisconsin Press, 1999.

6

Ethnicity

Ethnic cultures are some of the richest and most interesting in the world. The forms of culture – oral narrative, drama, song, music, visual image, and so on – are universal, but the specific content and the particular way the universal form is realized in any one situation, place, or time is highly varied and differentiated. And many of those differentiations can be attributed to the fact that people cluster together in communities often for reason of ethnic affiliation and identity.

Ethnicity is both a physical fact and a cultural creation. An ethnicity comes into being when a group of people intermarry and form a large extended family that lasts usually for centuries, if not millennia. An ethnicity in this sense is a group that shares certain genetic traits, and that sharing lasts so long as the pattern of intermarriage lasts. Ethnicity usually manifests itself as physical differences such as eye shape or skin color. And it is doubtful it is more than that. Conservative racist thinkers believe that external traits signify internal mental differences. In this way of thinking, groups like Asians are more industrious "by nature." Africans, in contrast, lack initiative for the same inevitable genetic reason. Liberal thinkers respond by noting that were this account of the world true, all Africans would be lacking in initiative and all Asians would be industrious. But that is not the case. They note as well that what economic class people grow up in, what educational resources are available to them, and what family culture they are born into makes a much greater difference for success in life than ethnicity. When cultural differences are removed from consideration, ethnic differences become negligible. No group is more industrious than another for reasons that can be said to be genetic or ethnic. Indeed, it is more likely the case that the particular culture of an economic class plays a greater role in determining what an ethnic group seems to be capable of or not, and such class cultural influence is simply a matter of money – who has it and who does not. It is the culture of the group that in a way creates the illusion that ethnicity is something other than a physical accident, almost as relevant as blonde hair, that only appears significant because of its repetition over time.

☆ Ethnicity is a genetic inheritance that embodies itself physically. But it is also a sign with cultural meaning that links to emotions such as fear and anger and actions such as lynching and genocide. Our skin color is not a flat physical object; it has meaning for us and for others in systems of cultural identification and demarcation, ways ethnic social groups have of assigning places and roles and distinct essences to other people in order to justify their subordination or their exclusion from access to scarce social resources. Ethnic violence is a legacy of humans' primitive origins in a world where resources were scarce and violence the only means of safeguarding access to them. Banding together with others in ethnic tribal alliances was necessary to secure individual survival and to guarantee access to resources because no laws existed, no institutions other than simple tribal ones. That conservative disposition to safeguard our group, be it ethnic, national, or social, is with us still, even though we have evolved more modern liberal institutions that treat everyone equally and that in principle transcend primitive ethnic tribal group behavior. A *citizen* can be anyone with a legal right; the term should not in principle apply to just one ethnic group. A parliament ideally represents all and gives all a voice in governance regardless of ethnic group identity. These liberal inventions help move human society beyond the jungle and into a more civil realm guided by liberal principles. Our primitive conservative disposition to safeguard our ethnic or tribal group by doing violence to other groups undermines these efforts at liberal modernization. That disposition appears in the midst of our modern lives as eruptions of hatred and murder, sometimes on a monumental scale as with the Jewish Holocaust perpetrated by conservatives in World War II or the genocide carried out by conservative Turkish nationalists against Armenians in 1915. But they also take the form of statistics such as the datum that 8,000 African Americans die of high blood pressure each year, an illness that is related to the effects of ongoing racialized economic partitioning in the US.

Modern liberal ideals of ethnic tolerance and diversity are taking hold in many places, but many ethnic-based societies exist where such ideals have yet to gain wide acceptance. Usually, this is the case because one ethnicity is dominant or in the much greater majority. In Japan, the Korean minority is stigmatized and excluded from positions of power in the society. Korean children, if they wish to be accepted by their peers, must attend Japanese schools and make Japanese their first language. They are made to feel ashamed of their Korean ethnic identity and culture. A similar movement on the part of conservatives in the US has sought to make English mandatory for foreign-born citizens. Such moves have the effect of making children feel stigmatized because of their ethnicity, and they turn that hatred from outside on themselves. Ethnic minorities, as a result, are usually characterized by higher levels of pathology, both physical and emotional, than the dominant population.

Ethnicity is also one of the languages with which we think about the world. And like so much of the information that circulates in the media and in everyday discourse (rumor, gossip, small talk, etc.), ethnic information is a mix of truth and inaccurate or incomplete representation. Indeed, the danger culture poses for the issue of ethnicity is that cultural representations exist on a spectrum from the objective and factual on the one end to the fictive and conjectural on the other. With cultural representation, we make fictions, but we use the same tools to make truths about the world, and the two often blend and mix in ways that can be harmful. To represent the world is to put an image between you and it, and such representations always risk being more fiction than fact. In the US, for example, Asian Americans have undergone a remarkable change of representational status. Often in the past, they were pictured in the popular imagination as an opium-ridden "yellow peril." As late as 1994, one could find a movie in American theaters – *Falling Down* – that used yellow-tinged backgrounds in scenes that stereotyped Asian Americans as animalistic, irrational, and anti-American.

More recently, Asian Americans have been pictured as nerdy over-achievers who are by nature smarter than others. The character of Harold in *Harold and Kumar Go to White Castle* is just such an academic over-achiever, a stereotype of the socially inept but innately intelligent Asian. Such an image arose in part because of stories in the media regarding the high number of young Asian Americans who were being accepted to highly competitive universities such as the University of California, Berkeley. While it is true that 38 percent of Asian Americans have college degrees in comparison to 20 percent for the White population, studies have shown that those numbers correlate with parents' level of economic success and level of education, a correlation that holds true for Whites as well. Asian Americans from poor backgrounds do not fare as well as Asian Americans from professional class background, and they do not fare better than Whites of any economic background. In other words, economic status plays a more significant role than ethnicity in determining academic success. More Asian Americans than in the past belong to the educated professional classes because of immigration policies. Restrictions on immigration in the twentieth century have meant that fewer working-class and more highly educated professional-class Asians have been allowed into the United States. The very competitive culture of achievement in this new immigrant group, not any innate ethnic trait or essence, accounts for their children's success. Like professional-class Whites, educated Asian American professionals have access to better schools. When one controls for socioeconomic background and educational level, there is in fact no difference between Whites and Asian Americans in regard to educational achievement.

Yet since the 1960s, and in response to the arguments many made then that endemic racism prevented especially African Americans from advancing in American society, Asian American have been presented by conservatives as a "model minority" who are different from African Americans in their level of achievement. This model minority of passive, industrious, non-troublemakers disproves the claim that conservative racism prevents African Americans from advancing out of widespread poverty, and they confirm the conservative belief that only individual initiative accounts for social standing. That ethnic argument is only true, however, of the professional class amongst Asian Americans. A greater percentage of Asian Americans than of White Americans live in poverty. In addition, although Asian Americans complete more years of schooling than Whites on average, they earn less income than comparable Whites, and they are comparatively under-represented in positions of power and authority in American politics and business. In other words, the model minority is truly a minority even within the Asian American ethnic group, and they are only model until they reach the workplace. There, the same conservative practices of exclusion and subordination that led to the construction of the cultural myth of the model minority as a way of blaming victims of racism for their own victimization turn on that very model minority. They become like the very Blacks whose exclusion they inadvertently helped to justify.

The cultural images by which we "know" other ethnic groups always do injustice to those groups simply by virtue of how such representations have to work. They cannot be as complex, as differentiated, or as specific as the ethnic group itself. Indeed, even by imaging those ethnic others as a "group," one begins the process of misrepresenting them. All ethnic groups are also divided internally by class and income level. Most are also divided geographically. Asian Americans, for example, come from a variety of places, all differentiated culturally – Japan, China, India, the Philippines, Vietnam, and so on. This problem with ethnic cultural representation become especially clear when one considers an industry like advertising that markets products often to specific ethnic groups like Latinos in the US. Latinos, like all ethnic groups, are not homogeneous. That is, they are not all the same or even similar. They come from different places (from Puerto Rico to Mexico) with different cultures. They belong to different income and social classes and are as differentiated as any other ethnic group in those terms. Yet advertising, in order to address them as a targeted market, must to a certain extent make a deliberate mistake and must assume they are in fact characterized by such a high degree of similarity within the ethnic group that they can be addressed in purely ethnic terms. They are assigned a uniformity they do not in fact possess.

This process of targeting entails two processes – identification and differentiation. First, Latinos are depicted as a uniform body of people with certain traits that all possess. Second, this ethnic cultural identity is portrayed as significantly different from other ethnicities, especially the dominant Anglo-American one. Advertising researchers characterize Hispanics as seeing themselves more in terms of their family and community than Whites. They supposedly have more respect for elders, and a sense of obedience is instilled in their children. They uphold hierarchical social roles, and men in the group are characterized by machismo or dominance behavior. These traits differentiate them from Whites who are portrayed as more individualistic, as relying more on themselves than on family, and as favoring democracy over hierarchy in social relations. While Whites are thought of as middle class, Hispanics are characterized more in terms of a common culture that overrides class differences.

For example, in a 1998 ad for AT&T's auto-redial feature on its telephones, a young Hispanic couple asks permission to marry, but the girl's father is absent. The boy asks for the girl's hand in marriage, and the girl's aunt says, "Only the hand." Next we see the girl dialing a phone using the redial feature to reach her father, who gives permission to marry. The ad emphasizes the supposed importance of traditional hierarchical family relationships in Hispanic culture. The children are not independent; they depend on the authority of elders to make important life decisions. In another ad from 1997 for ITT Technical Schools, young Hispanics, rather than be associated with individual striving, as Whites are in other ITT ads, are depicted thanking family and friends for helping them succeed.

The student's success is portrayed not as individual but as that of a role model for his community. Ads targeted to Hispanics also seek to balance a sense of attachment to one's geographic or cultural roots with a sense of the importance of participating in American culture. Hispanics in ads are portrayed as having a strong sense of tradition, and images often evoke homelands that have been left behind to come to the US. Miller Beer ads in the 1980s offered Hispanic customers familiar images of their lives – kids playing soccer, a *vaquero* riding in a rodeo, bands playing "Latin" instruments such as maracas, and so on. They also contained anthems that resembled Hispanic songs and that offered drinking Miller Beer as a new tradition one could acquire in America. The ads suggested that one could preserve one's "Latin lifestyle" while nevertheless melting into US culture: "Here where opportunity is so clear, when you know how to strive, and the family can be better off, without forgetting our roots. Here where one embraces with sincerity to seal friendships, you sing with joy here, you drink Miller ice cold. Miller is of this nation as we are full of heart. Clear and honest for all to see. Miller is of this great nation. Miller beer, purity and quality you can clearly see." Advertising can also be a way of stigmatizing traditional practices and of educating Latinos as consumers of modern goods that replace traditional ways of doing things. That is often the case with ads for such things as laundry detergent, which is presented as modern and a move away from the past. Now that one is in America, Fab detergent ads suggest, one should do things the American way. Such ads are part of a larger cultural campaign to render *Latinidad* or Latinness smoother so that a larger audience can be reached. People of Hispanic descent vary greatly in skin tone, from very dark to very light, the result of the mix of Spanish, African, and indigenous ethnic lines in South America. As a result, ads strive to present images of Hispanics that are neither too dark nor too light. And the Spanish that is spoken in such ads, similarly, is generic and unaccented and is presented as a standard that belongs to no one single linguistic community. In fact, it is upper-class Mexican Spanish which is supposedly without any mark of regional accents, especially from the Caribbean basin, but it is regional nevertheless.

Of course, advertisers are not entirely to blame for the way ethnic groups are represented as separable entities with distinct cultural traits. Such traits can be real; the question is how applicable are they to an entire group? Moreover, a sense of a separate group identity is encouraged and embraced by members of ethnic groups without coaching from advertisers. Some people define their identity in terms of their ethnic group at least in part.

Its achievements are their achievements. When a Hispanic radio station attained the number-one ranking in New York City, one Latina remarked, "It was about time. We are no longer an obscure force, we are finally being recognized. We are moving forward, and no one can stop us."

It should not be surprising that ethnic groups that live with other members of their group in boundaried geographic locations should share a culture – beliefs, practices, tastes, ideas, and ways of making cultural artifacts such as music. Indeed, one of the most common ways of locating music is to speak of it in such terms – Europop or Jamaican reggae. Yet musical culture has also always leaped across ethnic boundaries with alacrity. White rock was Black rhythm and blues. Modern broadcast media, from radio to Lime Wire, globalize certain kinds of music such as techno and trance and make them less recognizable as the products of a particular culture, especially an ethnic one. Some cultural music styles are resistant to such transportation; they retain too many ethnic markers or traits to be universally embraced, or they retain too many elements of traditional styling that seems outdated to young people, the primary makers and consumers of popular music. Mexican brass band music, Jewish Klezmer music, and Indian and Arabic vocals – all are potent forms within certain geographic boundaries or ethnic cultural boundaries, but they do not appeal to an international youth audience in the way that the Europop sound of a band like Ozone does. The very ethnic feel that makes them so valuable within a particular community obstructs access to a wider international community. Nevertheless, modified hybrids are possible, as when guitarist Django Reinhardt made gypsy music universally appealing by joining it to jazz and other musical forms.[1]

Certain ethnic cultural styles are valuable on the international scene, however, precisely because of elements that might be considered "ethnic." African American hip hop began to merge in New York City in the middle of the 1980s. At Black clubs, disk jockeys began to mix sounds instead of just playing numbers straight through. Armed with multiple turntables (for vinyl recordings), they "sampled" various kinds of music, mixing them into something entirely new. The dance forms that developed in response to the music were noticeable for their athleticism, and quickly, they spread to the streets as break dancing. Hip hop emerged within a particular urban African American community, but its distinguishing features – spoken poetry, street-wise identity performance, non-melodic rhythms, a shout-and-reply structure, and so on – were easily borrowable by non-members of the ethnic group, with the most successful being Eminem, a White man whose film, *8 Mile*, somewhat audaciously ups the ethnic ante by showing him defeating African American performers of the music he borrowed from them. Hip hop proved mobile internationally as well. In Japan, hip hop artists imitated American blacks in vocalization, dress, and hairstyle, but they also adapted and recoded the ethnic identity of the music, rendering "black" as "yellow" and combining hip hop rap forms with traditional Japanese instrumentation and music forms such as taiko drums and kabuki, a Japanese musical theatrical form. But the highly physical dancing style practiced by early male hip hop artists also helped to transform traditional male attitudes in Japan regarding such things as dancing. "I always thought dancing is something only women do," Crazy-A, one of Japan's first hip hop artists, once noted after seeing the movie *Flashdance* in 1983 and having tried to imitate the performance in the movie by Rock Steady Crew.

The adoption of hip hop also has its more problematic side, however. Japanese girls, who in recent years have taken to performing various identities such as Barbie Girls in a highly self-conscious, ironic way, took to tanning their skin dark brown in imitation of African American skin pigmentation. This *ganguro* or *face black* style lasted several years and inspired complaints about how "blackness" was being exploited in a way that seemed mildly racist. Some images of *ganguro* girls are online at http://www.japanguidebook.com/articles/weird-japanese-fashion-81.html.[2] Nevertheless, transnational hip hop foregrounded elements of Black American life such as urban poverty with which some Japanese artists could identify. Crazy-A grew up in the poor San'ya area of Tokyo, where people seeking day laborer jobs are common, and when he saw the hip hop movie *Wild Side* he could therefore easily relate to the bombed-out look of the New York represented in the movie. Like many of the boys who would become rap artists in America, he grew up fighting on the streets and being part of gang culture. But he and other hip hop artists report being saved from lives of crime by the discovery of the hip hop scene. It offered them a way of making a living and supporting a family.

Ethnic signs are clearly mobile and easily transported across ethnic cultures. Black American youth may have invented the style consisting of hoodies and beaked baseball caps, but Whites soon adopted it. The mobility of ethnic signs can lead to cultural forms such as satire that make fun of those very signs and of the ethnic-based attitudes that respond to such signs usually with fear and loathing. Sacha Baron Cohen has played his comic clown Ali G, for example, by dressing as a highly exaggerated, mock comic version of the White urban gangster wannabe and did fake interviews with famous political figures such as Newt Gingrich (a former US congressman). To some, Ali G might be offensive; he portrays White working-class urban youth as buffoons. But Cohen also uses the figure for critically satiric purposes.

Mobile ethnic signs can also become a form of currency especially in urban settings in the US where ethnic groups live close to one another and mix in schools especially. Because many Latin American immigrants are perceived as being "backward" by other youth, they seek to acquire "Blackness" by dressing, acting, and speaking like their African American schoolmates. In part this phenomenon has to do with the acquisition of urban competence, an ability to survive psychologically and socially in a terrain marked by hierarchy, exclusion, group identity, and coded languages. But it is also a traditional survival mechanism for immigrants that in the past took the form of "becoming White," of acquiring new names and of acquiring new forms of behavior and speech that shed all signs of one's immigrant ethnic roots. For many Latin American youth in places like Newark, New Jersey, becoming Black is the equivalent of becoming American.[3] They try not to appear Hispanic because "it's not the cool thing. You have to be hard, trying to be like, you know, a thug, and so they emulate that. Nobody wants to be White because that's Portuguese and so that's un-cool and even looked down upon." What study of the students in Newark high schools suggests is that kids can learn ethnicity by acquiring ethnic style. It is theatrical, a rehearsed and repeated role. A Puerto Rican girl recounts how "[a Portuguese girl] once said, 'I would have never thought in my life I would ever hang out with a Puerto Rican, because they're loud, obnoxious,' and you know. And it's true because all Puerto Ricans are loud [laughs]. Now she's different. Now she's loud like me and she likes it. I taught her how to really come out and be out-going." Some students who do not belong to one of the majority ethnic groups take pride in being integrated into those groups by learning their style. One girl from Cape Verde tells how she grew up entirely with Puerto Ricans "and when I got to high school all my close friends were Puerto Rican. My boyfriend is Puerto Rican too. I have more in common with Puerto Ricans, and when people look at me, how I dress, they think I am."

At the center of the high school culture of Newark, however, was the Black youth community. They hung out on the second floor of one of the high schools, which was called the "ghetto floor." The third floor was for immigrants, and the fourth for Brazilians. But many of these Hispanic kids yearned to be ghetto and cool. ""Because it's good to be ghetto, but you have to be classy ghetto, you know? I mean, it's okay to talk loud when you're with your friends. 'Yo, dawg, wassup?!!!' But some people get stupid and do this in class." Interestingly, however, the acquired role quickly becomes an identity of one's own, something integral to one's sense of self rather than a performed act. "The Puerto Ricans view the immigrant kids as corny, rural, you know. But even that doesn't last long. The immigrant kids pick up on the dress style and the mannerisms right away. And they don't say 'those are Black people's mannerism,' no. They say, 'those are *Puerto Rican* mannerisms.'" Interestingly, immigrant Brazilians, because they are associated with a well-known international urban cultural scene, are thought to already inhabit a "ghetto" of their own.

The Portuguese occupy a privileged position in this multiethnic community because they are White-skinned. Appearing White has been one way for excluded ethnic communities to gain an entry to power and affluence in America. The US has a history of *nativism*, the idea that only native-stock White Protestants are truly American. Broader, more multiethnic definitions of what it means to be an American citizen have emerged and been promoted in recent decades, but Whiteness, because it is linked to social power and to wealth, is still associated in the eyes of urban youth with an ideal of social status and consumption to which many of the youth aspire. The poorer can only afford fake Louis Vuitton handbags, but some aspire higher, and to appear White, they buy real Vuitton bags. "Like I know some Portuguese people who try to be all high class and whatever and in the inside they are poor. It's like you just as poor as me, 'cause you're right across the corner from me, in the townhouse next door. … They pay the real Louis Vuitton and then next thing you know they talk about being poor and how their mother can't pay rent. Go and explain." Differences of income clearly intersect with ethnic differences. One consequence is that multiculturalism, the ideal of an achieved mixture of social groups defined by ethnicity rather than by income, obfuscates the fact that economic inequality is a core feature of American life. And it often is linked to ethnic differences. The Black youths who are imitated by their Hispanic counterparts are also thought of by some teachers in the high schools of Newark as dangerous; "ethnic problems" in the school are blamed on them. They are linked to gang activity. To posit them as a model of ethnic style for immigrant youth is to acknowledge how they are driven by economic inequality and poverty to adopt practices (gang belonging) and ideals (toughness, criminality) that reinforce their exclusion from a White-dominated economy.

Student Exercise

Look at these ads targeted to Latinos and discuss whether or not they draw on ethnic stereotypes:

http://www.youtube.com/watch?v=yjkH6z53Rj4&feature=PlayList
&p=78056437A20A0981&index=2

http://www.youtube.com/watch?v=yjkH6z53Rj4&feature=PlayList
&p=78056437A20A0981&index=2

http://www.youtube.com/watch?v=RN30hc3ICUQ

Stuff White People Like is a popular blog that has landed a book deal for its author, and spawned a host of imitators (such as Stuff Iranians Like and Stuff Asians Like). The author of this blog details stereotypically White activities and gives tongue-in-cheek instructions on how to interact with White People. The author's tone makes it clear that this is self-conscious stereotyping (and other blogs state this clearly). But does such self-conscious stereotyping act to draw attention to the often ludicrous nature of ethnic stereotypes, or does it instead act to normalize these stereotypes, making them seem more accurate and applicable?

Stuff White People Like: http://stuffwhitepeoplelike.com
Stuff Iranians Like: http://stuffiranianslike.wordpress.com
Stuff Asian People Like: http://www.asian-central.com/
stuffasianpeoplelike/

The newspaper column *Ask a Mexican* by Gustavo Arellano addresses questions and comments about Mexican culture, as well as Hispanic culture at large. Arellano responds to readers' questions with a blend of English and Spanish slang, in essays that discuss topics from immigration and migrant workers, to the veneration of Tweety Bird. As a columnist and a public figure, Arellano has taken on the job of representing and explaining Mexican-ness. But what makes him suited to this responsibility? How does one become (or avoid becoming) representative of an entire ethnicity? Arellano is himself Mexican – does that mean that he is automatically qualified as an expert on Mexican ethnicity? If so, why is his viewpoint more valid than that of the Mexican readers who he often corrects in his column? If not, what differences are there between identifying with an ethnic group and representing an ethnic group, and what qualifies a person to do either?

Ask a Mexican: http://www.ocweekly.com/columns/view/3246

Notes

1. Wikipedia, "Django Reinhardt," http://en.wikipedia.org/wiki/Django_Reinhardt (accessed October 8, 2009).
2. Japan Guidebook, "Weird Japanese Fashion," http://www.japanguidebook.com/articles/weird-japanese-fashion-81.html (accessed October 8, 2009).
3. All of the following quotes from Newark, NJ, high school students are from the author's own research.

Sources

On Asian Americans as a "model minority," see Stacy Lee, "Behind the Model-Minority Stereotype: Voices of High-and Low-Achieving Asian American Students," *Anthropology & Education Quarterly* 25, no. 4 (December 1994): 413–429; David Crystal, "Asian Americans and the Myth of the Model Minority," *Social Casework* 70, no. 7 (September 1989): 405–413; and Doobo Shim, "From Yellow Peril through Model Minority to Renewed Yellow Peril," *Journal of Communication Inquiry* 22, no. 4 (1998): 385–409. On ethnic advertising, see Arlene M. Davila, *Latinos, Inc* (Berkeley, Calif., 2001). On Newark high school culture, see Jean Anyon, "Race, Social Class, and Educational Reform in an Inner-City School," *Teachers College Record* 97, no. 1 (1995): 69–94.

7

Identity, Lifestyle, and Subculture

Who we are as individual beings – our "identity" – is bound up with the culture we live in. Although it is something outside us, culture makes its way into us through our eyes and ears. We learn the languages of culture as we grow up – what particular kinds of clothes "mean," for example, or what particular actions are good or bad or what words and attitudes are appropriate or not in what situations. We also acquire ways of understanding and methods of reasoning that we use to read the cultural world around us. We see and know the meaning of a host of things – objects, events, and institutions – because we internalize rules, grammars, and conventions from the culture we grow up in. All of these ways of seeing, reading, and assessing the world around us become part of who we are. If you grow up in rural Wisconsin and engage in the culture of hunting, road sign stealing, Saturday night drinking in crowded cars while listening to country music, and working in auto assembly plants, you are more likely to see Hillary Clinton as a threat to civilization as you know it and Sarah Palin as the way a well-lipsticked lady is supposed to look and be. You are less likely to embrace or endorse the cultural ideals and political ideas that are current in more urban settings such as the Upper West Side of Manhattan, a location more likely to be populated by highly educated professionals whose culture includes evenings at the Kennedy Center listening to classical music. Growing up in rural Wisconsin, you will be less likely to identify with someone very different from yourself like Barack Obama.

None of us exist outside cultural immersion of this sort. We all learn to see and feel and think from our culture in certain ways. We all acquire an internal identity from outside ourselves. What we are inside ourselves is shaped in part by what is outside of us. Although I come from Ireland, I have lived long enough in American culture to be aware of its languages and its dictionaries. My cultural identity is more American than Irish by this point. I can spot someone who is "corporate" and distinguish him or her from someone who appears "countercultural" quite easily because I have learned to recognize the cultural signs of each identity while growing up in America over the past several decades. I've learned the dictionary that allows the meaning of those signs – blue jeans, loose sweater, and a colorful neck scarf as distinguished from blue suit, red tie, and very neat hair – to be read, recognized, and deciphered.

Near where I live is a town called Madison that many characterize as "corporate," and further down the coast is a town called Guilford that is characterized as "countercultural." In Madison, you will see more Mercedes and BMWs, cars that indicate high levels of wealth that is usually associated with the lifestyle of those who work in business. In Guilford, you are more likely to see cars associated with middle-class incomes, many of them older Volvos or other family cars. Madison has more upscale clothing shops and galleries that sell original paintings – all signs of the presence of people with money. In a very small sign of the same culture, if you go to the public library, you will be more likely to see elegantly dressed older women with carefully done gray hair whose reading glasses are held in place with decorative and expensive-looking neck bands. In Guildford, in contrast, you will be more likely to see a children's toy store and a bakery cafe that looks distinctly "hippyish," a leftover or a deliberate evocation of the counter-cultural world of the 1960s. This is the home to people with families who are probably more liberal politically than the slightly older group that clusters in Madison.

Each place thus has a distinct culture defined in part by the identities of the people who live there. In each place, people do the same physical things each day, but they also lead slightly different lifestyles. In Madison, people are more likely to have leisure or be retired with wealth to live on. They shop or read books during the day rather than work; they might engage in philanthropy to keep busy. They spend so much on books that the local privately owned bookstore – one of the few left that is not part of a chain – can afford to bring in authors for readings. For sports, the inhabitants of Madison prefer golf to the National Basketball Association. Madison has its own first-run movie theater, a small place that specializes in unique independent or foreign films. It is for people with "higher" or more educated tastes. Guilford has more middle-class people, and the theater nearby is of the usual American kind – all first-run American films. It also has a hardware store, something you would not see in Madison, where people are less likely to do home repairs themselves, although Guilford has a wine shop, a token of a lifestyle that again might be more countercultural in that it suggests the presence of people who enjoy a European conception of the pleasures of life. The conservative Protestants of Madison would probably be less inclined to be sybarites, people who take pleasure in physical taste, because their Protestant religion encourages self-control as a sign of virtue. You would be more likely to see a Catholic church in Guilford because more working-class Irish- and Italian-descended people would live there. They tend to be middle as opposed to upper class and would be found in fewer numbers in the much more expensive Madison, where houses values are decidedly higher because there is more money bidding for them. Housing prices help to keep the population of the town relatively homogeneous. Middle-class Irish people cannot afford to live there.

Ethnic terms are often applied to certain cultures, and that is true of Madison, where the people who cluster there are often characterized as *WASPs*, or White Anglo-Saxon Protestants. This social group is the longest-standing European descended ethnic group in the US. For a long time, their culture was equated with "American" culture. Their religious, social, economic, and political beliefs and assumptions formed an ideological core, reinforced through government institutions and social policies, that remained in place in the US for several centuries. Those beliefs were linked to a particular lifestyle and they fostered particular kinds of identities – ways of feeling, thinking, speaking, and behaving. WASPs, when they were ascendant, believed that their religion was superior to all others, and they sought therefore to "convert" others to Protestant Christianity. One could say they were arrogant and insensitive to the diversity of beliefs. But this arrogance had its humorous side. When in 1876, they sponsored an international gathering of religions (with the hidden agenda of converting them all to Protestantism), the Protestant ministers were surprised to be confronted with equally zealous attempts to convert them to the one right religion, which of course was Hinduism.

The same sense of superiority or arrogance appeared in other dimensions of WASP culture. They looked down on other ethnic groups who were not as economically successful because they had less inherited wealth or who came to America with little other than their ability to labor. WASPs were notoriously defensive of property (a WASP friend once remarked that the WASP drug of choice was real estate). This attitude made them reluctant to agree to measures that would assure economic fairness in America; they supported the violent suppression of labor unions, for example, in the nineteenth century and fought to make sure their property was not taken in the form of taxes to support poor people, a group WASPs perceived as lacking in good attitudes toward work, during the Great Depression. That was the case because WASPs believed strongly in the idea that one's success in life depended on personal virtues such as industriousness and thrift. A core belief of WASP culture was that economic success was not a token of being better connected through school and family ties but rather of being more in possession of essential virtues that guaranteed success to those who possessed them. WASPs were therefore also hostile to ways of thinking that looked at society as a whole made up of interrelated parts because such explanations (scornfully referred to as *theory*) drew attention to the fact that economic success depended on one's inheritance, one's connections, one's good fortune in education, and other non-personal factors. Virtue was often in the eyes of "theory" an effect or result of such things as inherited wealth and good social position at birth than of personal traits. One could afford to be thrifty if one was not starving, but not if one had a family to feed and very low income.

A typical WASP lifestyle confirmed the group's beliefs. They attended church regularly and formed a community with other like-minded church-goers. They frequented certain kinds of cultural events that connoted "high culture" such as the orchestra or the theater, and that confirmed their sense of possessing superior taste in cultural matters. They collectively engaged in volunteerism and philanthropy; giving away wealth in small amounts was perceived to be a token of virtue. But WASPs were also notoriously exclusive. They were associated with private clubs where golf, a physically undemanding sport for "gentlemen," could be played in serene settings, and such clubs often had rules forbidding membership by other ethnic groups such as Jews. The ideal of personal virtue also took a toll in that it entailed self-control and the suppression of passionate behavior that was construed as a sign of a lack of virtue, of being too much the prisoner of feeling rather than moral self-discipline. WASP men often therefore appeared emotionless and even coldhearted. Perhaps as a result, hard alcohol, which quickly loosens reserve and makes conversation easier between reserved people, was associated with WASP business culture especially (in the form of the infamous two-martini lunch of the 1930s through the 1960s). In the *Thin Man* comedies of the 1930s, one sees the self-image of the WASP as the cutely tipsy gentleman who has had "a few too many."

WASPs as a cultural group draw attention to the difference between mainstream or dominant cultures and subcultures. Dominant cultures usually work because they are not associated with any one group or any one particular interest. The culture and the culture's rules especially sup-posedly apply to all equally. But that is only true of very homogeneous cultures such as Japan, where one ethnic group, isolated from mixture on an island can end up identified with the nation's entire culture (to the great detriment of ethnic minorities such as Koreans). In America, the main-stream or dominant culture for a long time was WASP culture; they formed a homogeneous group that controlled the nation's economy and its politi-cal life. But there were always interlopers coming through the open door (so that WASPs become associated with closing the door to immigration over time). Irish political radicals, chased out of Ireland by the English after a failed revolt against English colonization in the late eighteenth century, were one of the first to challenge WASP cultural authority. They spoke in ways that WASPs felt were inappropriate, for one thing, using polemic instead of genteel, self-controlled speech in journalism, and they proposed modifications to the settled social order that were disturbing of the idea that virtue and property ownership were linked naturally to one another. But the identification of a particular social group's culture with the entirety of American culture (so that that group's norms became everyone's norms in the form of such things as rules of etiquette that distinguished civilized people from ill-mannered people, usually along class lines) endured into the twentieth century. All other ethnic or class cultures were considered subordinate to the WASP ideal of genteel speech, proper behavior, and good manners.

The word *subculture* connotes a culture within a larger mainstream culture. With time, WASPs have become a subculture in America because the mainstream has expanded to include the cultural preferences of many other social groups, and to a degree, WASPs always were a subculture that managed through sheer social status to make their particular worldview dominant and universal, something that seemed to apply to everyone in American society. The inappropriateness of that assumption became especially clear when Native Americans were asked in the late nineteenth century (by a law called the Dawes Act) to give up their own more com-munitarian culture and to adopt the lifestyle and the cultural norms of the WASP elite; they were forbidden to wander and hunt and were given farms and tools and told to become "striving individuals" who would succeed by learning the WASP virtues of industriousness, thrift, and moral self-control. The experiment failed because WASPs forgot that the cultural inheritance they relied on to supply them with those virtues from outside was not present in Indian life. WASPs made the mistake of assuming their own virtues arose from within themselves and that they would arise from within Native Americans if they were given the chance to cultivate them. Some immigrant groups, on the other hand, sought to "pass" as WASPs by adopting the names and the lifestyle associated with WASP culture.

The study of modern subcultures at first focused on youth subcultures in Britain. Youth, especially adolescence, is an inventive and creative time in many people's lives. Emerging into adulthood, young people have supple minds and lively imaginations, and they are not yet required by the world of work to conform to prevailing standards of dress in order to be success-ful and to earn a living. Clothing and behavior standards do apply, of course, but they are not hard-wired to economic survival, and youth can enjoy a greater tolerance toward wildness of dress than adults, whose dress is more likely to be interpreted as a sign of character or of dispositions required for professional responsibilities. Indeed, such subcultural prac-tices on the part of youth as wildness of dress and nonconformity in regard to musical taste can be disruptive of conventions that enforce conformity. They can even disrupt more overt attempts at censorship by authoritarian governments, as the Chinese government discovered when it attempted to suppress a particular kind of televised youth music show that nevertheless reappeared in other venues after being banned from the airwaves. Eventually, the government was obliged to relent, and the popular shows became the basis of Cosplay, a major cultural form adopted from Japan for young people who dress up in various parts and perform on stages.[1]

The first studies of subcultures were concerned with their rebellious character. Subcultural style in dress, body decoration, behavior, and music was seen as a way of affirming a sense of value in the face of a dominant culture that treated working-class youth as if they had no value (especially in England's more class-stratified society). The "meaning of style" in sub-cultures such as punk in the 1970s was precisely that it allowed working-class youth to make meaning of their otherwise rather economically blighted lives. The music was appropriate for kids who could hardly afford to buy instruments like guitars let alone take expensive music lessons. It emphasized amateur discordance and was deliberately unprofessional. Subcultures provide an identity to participants in the subcultural lifestyle by demarcating them from other social groups that are often perceived to be dated, conservative, conformist, and mainstream. Often that main-stream is itself the residue of a subculture that has lost its allure and useful-ness or that belongs to another generation slightly older than the new subculture's participants. Punk, for example, came into being in difference from the musical and personal identity style of heavy metal, which had come to dominate popular music in the early to mid-1970s. Groups such as Led Zeppelin and Emerson, Lake, and Palmer were perceived by the young people who became punks as much too professional in musical style. Their music could not be learned or practiced by beginners because it entailed enormously expensive stage shows that few save the supergroups could afford. The music of groups such as Queen and the Moody Blues literally required orchestras. The lads who hung out at the SEX shop on Kensington Road in London wanted nothing of this. They rejected the long draping locks and ornate clothing of the heavy metallers and glam rockers, and instead emphasized a more rowdy and rough look that took the form of tight, ill-fitting clothing and homemade ornamentation such as safety pins. Rather than pleasing orchestral music, they made music that deliberately hurt the ears and offended mainstream taste. They embraced the radical politics of anarchism.

Punk was unique in its extremity at least initially, and it followed a trajectory over time that is common to such subcultures. Eventually, punk clothing was sold by the same clothing chains that were initially rejected by the punks, and punk style became mainstream. The Sex Pistols gave way to the Clash, a much more recognizably professional group of musicians. The punk preference for black clothing persisted into a new subculture called Goth in the 1980s. Underground music, especially in such US music scenes as Washington, DC, preserved the loud aggressive radicalism of original punk, but like heavy metal, it too spawned a reaction. In the mid-1980s, young people began to prefer softer sounds and lyrics that explored emotions. MTV branded this music "Emo," and around it grew up a subculture with the usual mix of affiliative elements that bond people together and make them feel part of a shared community and dissociative elements that differentiate them from those around them.

"Emo kids" wear their hair long in front and comb off to one side. A base of straightened black hair is often streaked with exuberant colors such as magenta and green. Add tight jeans, white belts, and hoodies (borrowed from African American hip hop culture), and you have a "typical" Emo kid. Like other subcultures, Emo is characterized by a particular style of thought and feeling that gives expression to aspects of the lives of young people. If punk expressed the class rage of poor English kids, Emo draws on the heightened emotionality of people who are experiencing particular kinds of feelings strongly for the first time and for whom some of those emotions can be quite overwhelming. Emo reaches especially toward despair and unhappiness, the feeling many young people have of "not fitting in" or of being alienated from their contemporaries. They feel deeply a sense of unhappiness at not being recognized or accepted, celebrated, or cherished. Adolescence is famous for being one of the most difficult passages in life; not surprisingly, some people kill themselves before reaching the end of the passage. Emo kids are sometimes into cutting, taking razors to their own skin in a version of the despair that gets expressed in suicide. Such despair arises out of a sense that one somehow does not count. Here is one account by an Emo kid of his reasons for cutting:

> [I]t sucks so much i finaley stopped took me a year my parents thout i had stoped but i just cut farther up my arm so they couldnt see but rubber bands are helpfull and i cut becouse my parents would fight constently and my sis would say how much of a loser i was and my friends stoped talking to me and my grandpa had open heart surgery almost whent rong he is a big part of my life so i was scared of loosing him. nothing has changed other than my grandpa my whole family sucks my parents think im crazy now but yep i dont care any more.[2]

After being told to get help, he replied,

> HELP only HELPS if you're able to get help. and no, i don't mean that it is physically impossible for me to get help … it's more complex than that. I want help … NEED help, but help means having to tell someone i'm not sure i trust. reason for the lack of trust: telling them would result in them informing people i REALLY don't want to know (ie. my grandma, sister, mom …) because i care about said people too much to have them worried about ME. I don't want people to worry about me. … A false sense of "happiness" is better than a genuine sense of sadness when it comes to OTHER people. I'm NOT playing a martyr. I just SERIOUSLY don't like it when people worry about a piece of worthless filth like myself.[3]

One can see why favorite Emo posters contain slogans such as "Pain doesn't hurt when it's all you've ever felt," "Lost in a world of hate," and "I don't need sex; life fucks me whenever it can." Or why a favorite Emo song might be called "Beautiful Sadness." Or why a typical Emo poem might be called "Fragile":

> Some people say your pathetic sitting in the corner on your own
> When all you want is time to reflect and be alone …
> Why is it that people put you down and make you feel so weak

When you want to hold your boyfriends hand but his friends don't think
   your good enough? ...
When you feel there is nothing left in this cruel world for you
Just stop and think your not the only one there is other people too
Look in the mirror and smile at what you have got
Dont be as fragile anymore dont, look at what your not![4]

That the Emo subculture generates hostility from other adolescents who do not share the affiliative values, ideas, and lifestyle is suggestive of what subcultures in general accomplish. A typical anti-Emo joke goes like this: "How many Emo kids does it take to change a light bulb? Three. One to do the replacing and two to write a poem about how much they miss the old one." Subcultures like Emo differentiate and lend distinction to a particular marked identity, one that stands out from the prevailing standard and norm. Such acts of differentiation generate hostility because they cast doubt on the standards that others use to define their own identities. And humans by nature react negatively to threats to their selves, be those threats physical or symbolic. The sense of devaluation and even of annulment that occurs symbolically or culturally is as threatening, it seems, as the possibility of physical harm. It is that same threat that probably impels young people to band together for protection in like-minded groups that place the danger the anonymity of the crowd represents in abeyance. One preserves one's sense of self by being able to have a self that others recognize and identity with. Oddly, by the logic of subcultural identity making, one gains a self not by expressively generating something entirely unique and specific to oneself from inside oneself but rather by adopting and adapting oneself to styles and images that come from outside. One becomes recognized as a self by being "one of us."

Subcultures are not unique to young people. One of the most persistent kinds of subculture over the ages was gay and lesbian. In response to the conservatism that came to dominate European society in the nineteenth century after the suppression of the French Revolution and the reforms in authoritarian conservative society it sought to bring about, a bohemian subculture came into being that evolved a different set of values, ones that were more liberatory in regard to natural impulses that conservatives sought to control or suppress, that indulged a taste for drug-induced experiences that opened up the imagination and transcended the brute positivism (knowledge based solely on easily verifiable facts) that made sure conservative society survived by cutting off speculation about alternatives, and that espoused radical ideals of social and economic equality at odds with "bourgeois" society's favoring of the rich over the poor at all times. Bohemianism was a lifestyle that embodied itself in dress, preferences in art and literature, and forms of cultural expression such as dance. If the bourgeoisie was repressive and repressed, bohemians were free thinkers, free spirits, and free lovers who shocked mainstream taste with their preference for openness and honesty regarding sexuality and human relations. If the bourgeois wore suits, the bohemians wore baggy loose clothing. If the bourgeois sought wealth above all, the bohemians were more interested in ephemeral beauty and the experience of life, heightened if at all possible with alcohol and drugs. They took seriously Walter Pater's maxim in the famous conclusion to his book *The Renaissance* to "burn always with this hard gem-like flame" of passionately experienced living.

Any group that is enjoined or denied entry into public life becomes a subculture. Jews are in some respects a classic example of a subculture – perhaps along with gays, one of the very first subcultures. Banned, excluded, they banded together, dressed alike, and developed affiliations and alliances, and their subcultural behavior served its function well; they survived. The same was true of anarchists in the nineteenth century. Where the dominant or mainstream culture is repressive or intolerant of difference, subcultures tend to form. Subculture usually conjures the idea of dissent and dissonance for this reason. They usually are at odds with dominant cultures that are conservative, that favor the repression of natural impulses, that promote unfairness and inequality, that rely on power, authority, and force to exert discipline on or control over others so that resources can be monopolized by a minority, that are anti-intellectual and suspicious of imagination or theoretical speculation of any kind, and the like. It is for this reason that one should distinguish a subculture like Emo, which allows those not favored by a dominant conservative picture of the world that endorses force and violence over care and empathy, that is hard-nosed realist instead of creative and imaginative, and that is repressive of life rather than celebratory of it, to feel that their values have a place in the world, from a conservative culture such as the hunting, beer-swilling, reactionary one of backwoods America. The latter in the eyes of Cultural Studies is not a subculture but a part of the cultural mainstream that most subcultures would be at odds with. In Cultural Studies, then, the "sub" in *subculture* connotes dissent and dissonance, something at odds with conservatism and with the conservative ideal of a society ruled by the tough and the thoughtless for the purposes of material accumulation by a minority. That core conservative value spreads itself out through a culture like that of America and is evident in everything from a militarist foreign policy when in conservative hands to the ideal of masculine toughness and group homogeneity in high schools. Whether the dissent is with the large idea or its small local permutation, it is dissent nevertheless. It is subculture.

Student Exercise

Go to the following website which lists Japanese subcultures:

http://tvtropes.org/pmwiki/pmwiki.php/Main/SubculturesInJapan

Pick one of the subcultures to research further. What are its distinguishing characteristics? How is it a "typical" subculture? What makes it a subculture? How would you compare it with subcultures in your own country?

Notes

1. Cosplay.com, Home page, http://www.cosplay.com (accessed October 10, 2009).
2. Luv-emo.com, "Luv-emo Forum," http://www.luv-emo.com/forum/forums. html (accessed October 10, 2009).
3. Luv-emo.com, "Luv-emo Forum."
4. Ibid.

Sources

On WASPs, see Eric Frank Russell, *Wasp* (New York, 1957); Peter Schrag, *The Decline of the Wasp* (New York, 1971); James Hunt, *The Evolution of Social Wasps* (New York, 2007); and Sally Clark, *Wasps* (Vancouver, BC, 2007). On subcultures, see Dick Hebdige, *Subculture: The Meaning of Style* (London, 1979); Steve Redhead, *Subculture to Club Culture: An Introduction to Popular Cultural Studies* (Oxford, 1997); and Ken Gelder, *The Subcultures Reader* (New York, 2005). On Emo, see http://www.luv-emo.com.

8

Consumer Culture and Fashion Studies

I have argued that our identity is both something in us – a cluster of feelings, ideas, assumptions, perceptions, and values – as well as something that happens to us as we live in the world. The world tells us who we are by assigning us roles at certain points in life – son or daughter, brother or friend, husband or wife, father or mother, manager or employee. Each of those roles imprints a new version of an identity on us, a new set of rules and expectations for thought, feeling, and behavior. Within each of those roles, we construct variable kinds of identity based on our capacities, our talents, and our experience. And our identities determine how we think about the world and how we act in it. Between that inner self and that outer world are language, bodily action or gesture, and dress and adornment. Our inner identity expresses itself through each one of those avenues of public representation.

Clothing expresses who you are in symbolic form that is also functional. To say it is "symbolic" is to say that it presents to the world a visual image of a quality of your inner being, and one possible quality might be your desire to be part of a social group or to identity with a cultural ideal you admire and desire to adopt for yourself. To say it is "functional" means that it has a practical purpose or use in relation to the world in which you live. When I go to my office to work as a university administrator, I have a choice between dressing formally – suit, tie, and dress shoes – or informally – no tie, sweater instead of suit, and casual shoes. I opt for the latter style more often than not because I favor comfort over formality, and I think a lot of rules regarding formality of dress in work situations are not justifiable. They belong to an older, more traditional world, and I tend to be someone who challenges and changes old rules. My identity is that of someone who takes issue with rules rather than following them blindly. That inner feeling, that part of my identity, expresses itself in my style of dress at work. But I also dress more formally when I have to present a different "face" to job candidates, for example, and seem more official. Then, I have a different role from that of the office worker who prefers comfort to formality.

Clothing also registers how your particular culture imprints itself on you from outside, shaping your style of dress and adornment as well as your inner identity. Our identities are often shaped by the rules, conventions, and expectations of society regarding proper behavior. We adapt ourselves to those external influences as we grow up in a particular society. That part of your identity that is assigned to you by the world or that you inherit from your culture also assumes the form of clothing and adornment style. Our clothing records our place in the world around us. It tells us who we are in relation to others and in relation to the institutions in which we work and live or with which we interact in our daily lives. That has always been the case, even in societies in which fashion is minimalist. The Koyapu, for example, a tribe in New Guinea that wears little in the way of clothing except sheaths or small cloths to cover the penis and the pudendum, have highly differentiated societies whose distinctions of rank register in differences in style of dress and adornment. Different kinds and colors of feathers distinguish women according to their place in the society's hierarchy, as do differences in the permissible size of the mouth plate which fits between men's teeth and their lower lip, pushing it out. The large plates are reserved for older men of high rank. Such differences in rank are important because they are associated with real differences in power in the society and in differences in access to the society's resources.

Our own modern societies are no different. Those of "high" rank, that is, those with access to more wealth than others, dress in a particular way that is reflective of their greater power and status. Mostly men, they wear expensive suits made of the finest materials and crafted by expert tailors. Look at a news photo of the Davos gathering of world economic leaders, and you will see men of this rank and clothing style. But look too at a range of popular magazines for men, from *GQ* and *Forbes* to *Guns & Ammo* and *Motor Trend*. What you will see is both a social range and a sartorial (or clothing) range in the photos and the advertisements. One can assume, I think, that the first two magazines are directed to high-income members of the business community, people with an interest in the financial information that *Forbes* provides and with the high-end fashion tips that younger members of the corporate community, especially men looking for mates and therefore interested in how they look to the opposite sex, might need. The second type of magazine is linked to activities and regions of the country usually associated with men in a lower-income range. What you will see is a difference between the elegant style that wealth supports and the somewhat more workaday and functional style associated with less wealth and with more practical needs than display for the purpose of impressing others or with attracting the opposite sex. Rather than Valentino, Carhartt.

If a man who usually wears Carhartt with his hunting friends suddenly showed up in an Yves St. Laurent suit, he would raise eyebrows and probably provoke laugher. We often use clothes as a way of expressing solidarity with a particular social or cultural group, for example, by dressing the same as them, or we distinguish ourselves from other groups or from particular values by dressing in a particular way that is strikingly at odds with the other group's style. One of the most resonant and obvious examples of such a use of fashion emerged in Black hip hop clothing styles over the past several decades. Initially, Black youth reached upward in American sartorial culture, borrowing a particular style from White clothing – the Tommy Hilfiger brand that was associated with the preppy or college preparatory school lifestyle. The adoption of Hilfiger by Black hip hop artists initially and then eventually by Black youth in general was ironic, but it also expressed a desire to overcome a social and economic class difference, registered in clothing styles, that symbolically embodied the exclusion of Black youth from White educational culture and the wealthy White leisure lifestyle. For Black youth, Hilfiger was a way of buying in symbolically to a world that in reality excluded them.

Not all sartorial meaning is expressive of inner identity or of group solidarity or group exclusion. Some meanings are assigned by other social groups. When I was growing up in the early to mid-1960s, there were two distinct social groups and two distinct clothing styles adopted by each group. The preppies wore penny loafers (yes, with pennies in them) and brown to light-colored clothing with traditional styling. Blue jeans were not yet fashionable, and they would have appeared too informal to this group. Mostly, these kids were middle class and aspired to go to college. On the other side were greasers. If the preppies wore their hair down in their face in imitation of the Beatles, the greasers used oil and combed their hair back, with a peak in front and a "duck back" look behind in imitation of mid-1950s Elvis and a host of imitators. Their clothing style was dramatically different – black leather jackets with tight black dress slacks and white shirts. They looked, quite deliberately, like hoodlums. It was all show, of course; they were some of the sweetest people in the world and were touching because they were working class and poor for the most part, but they needed to do something dramatic in terms of dress to add some value to their lives, some sense of being distinct. They were also of course assuming for themselves a sartorial armor that gave them an aura of toughness that fended off the implicit insult that came their way from a culture that favored economic success as an index of personal worth. While the meaning of their style of dress for themselves was solidarity with others like them as well as with images of "outsiders" from 1950s movies such as *Rebel without a Cause*, the meaning it was assigned by the larger society was more sinister. In school movies about proper dress and behavior, greaser girls were usually depicted as "sluts" who wore pants that were much too tight and blouses that were much too revealing of flesh. Movies of the era depicted them as dangers to society, petty criminals who needed discipline and control.

Mediating these practices of stylistic initiative, invention, and imitation is the concept of "cool." Cool is both a cultural concept that implies a comfortable stasis, a sense of being at home with oneself in a calm space of one's own defining that sets one apart from others and from external influences that bedevil others, and a mechanism of cultural activity in the form of a mobile ideal of what is fashionable and what should be imitated so that one is oneself as cool as the first ones to adopt that fashion style. Someone begins the process by, for example, starting to wear Tommy Hilfiger sweatshirts in ostentatious ways that set them apart from others who have not yet "caught on" to the new style and the new ideal of cool. Because cool implies a constantly process of setting oneself apart from others in a new cool identity that is different, it serves well a fashion industry that thrives on mutability and permanent sales that guarantee income for owners of the industry. The industry must, however, keep on top of that mutability, and so "cool hunters" such as the L Report are hired to seek out new styles and try out new products on the streets of cities like New York. Here is what the L Report says of itself on its website:

Today's consumers, regardless of age or income, aspire to style and prestige like never before. The L Report® is the leading global source for style and prestige insight, with more than a decade of experience in uncovering emerging cultural movements. Data is sourced from Lambesis' exclusive network of Urban Pioneers™, style and prestige experts in cities across the globe, as well as an online panel of style and prestige influencers.[1]

Web sites and blogs such as http://www.thecoolhunter.net/ and http://www.complex.com/blogs/2009/01/06/street-detail-canadas-cool-hunter/ also track changes in cool style.[2]

Fashion is thus a complex nexus of self-identity, social influence, cultural ideal, and commercial industry. To the degree that we all belong to a social or ethnic group or to an economic class, our shopping tastes will be shaped by the particular social world in which we grow up and live. Our tastes will correspond to our class location, and our ability to buy certain kind of clothing, for example, will be shaped as well by that economic context. Poor people, for example, have much less money to spend on clothes, and they must think of clothes in more practical terms than wealthy people, who can afford to change fashions each season. Functionality or practicality is an important consideration for the poor in buying clothes. The wealthy can afford to focus more on impractical considerations such as aesthetics and status display. Indeed, their clothes – when worn at "gala" events such as philanthropy dinners – have meanings that have little to do with their practical usefulness as garments that cover one's body. They symbolize wealth and "taste," an awareness of what is most "fashionable" in dress.

The wealthy also shop in different locations than poor people. While the poor may go to Walmart in search of cheap imitations of high-end designer clothes, which use poor-quality artificial materials made with inexpensive and hasty stitching, the wealthy will shop at Neiman-Marcus and do not mind paying three to ten times as much for certain things that might be gotten more cheaply elsewhere. Imitation and aspiration play a large role in shopping. We aspire to be considered part of a higher status group, even though our income may not justify membership, and we execute those aspirations by purchasing cheaper versions of more expensive goods. Those goods have status value for us largely for intangible reasons – the aura a designer name inspires, for example, in the eyes of others in our social universe. But the things themselves are easily imitated with exactly the same materials and quality of workmanship, as the numerous knock-offs of designer handbags for women attest. They cost very little and look exactly like the much more expensive originals. What this suggests is that the value of things – how they look to others especially – becomes our own value, our own sense of worth. We feel better when others look at us, envy us, and aspire to be as high status as us.

High-end designer fashion brings together art and economics. Designers seek minor differentiations of dress that continually distinguish the clothing of an elite who can afford to spend a great deal of money on things whose duration may be quite short from the mass market, ready-to-wear clothing of everyone else. Because such high levels of creativity go into designer clothes, they have a perfectly non-economic claim to superiority and often set the example for mass market clothing. But popular clothing culture also is a realm of creativity, and the two often vie with one another. Punk clothing style established black as the color to imitate before designers could catch up, and when designers decided longer dresses were "in" as a way of displacing the mini-skirts of the 1960s, women in the 1970s refused to go along and chose "hot pants" instead. But designers were successful in pillaging a gypsy style for women in the 1990s that emphasized loose skirts with folds, dramatic dark color contrasts, sweater jackets, and long scarves from the arts counterculture and turning it into a mainstream style.

Consumer culture is necessarily bound up with economic life, and given that the kind of economic life we humans have so far constructed for ourselves is one that depends on a circle of production and consumption in which the second term plays a crucial role in sustaining the first (which in turn sustains life on earth through payment for work), the link between consumption and economic life is worth attending to. As usual with economics, a fair amount of self-interested unfairness immediately grabs one's attention, from the sweat shops of underpaid laborers in Southeast Asia that produce clothing for high-income consumers elsewhere to the underpaid deliverers of consumer services such as Starbucks coffee in advanced economic settings like North America and Europe. Something as apparently simple as sugar in English tea had behind it a reality of African slavery in the sugar-growing region of the world. And a struggle continues to establish "fair trade" rules that will assist commodity growers in getting a fairer price on the world market for their goods.

Advertising is central to consumer culture. It consists of a mixture of rhetoric, theater, and visual design. It is rhetorical because it makes an

appeal in language to an audience it seeks to influence in some way –
usually to buy something. It is theatrical because, as television commercials
especially, it tells stories or enacts fictional scenes that make a point and
serve the rhetorical purpose of the advertisement. And it consists of visual
design because it must arrest the attention of the audience and make it look
at something appealing and meaningful. Print and televisual ads are objects
that can be analyzed into their component features – image, narrative, text,
mode of address, implied cultural context, and so on. And it can be located
within a context of production and reception that supplies it with
interpretable meaning. For an ad to be complete, it must use cultural
schemes and signs that are compatible with perceptual schemes the target
audience has ready to use in interpreting it. The signs an ad uses take
meaning from the surrounding culture. Images of a Black basketball super-
star such as Michael Jordan are immediately meaningful to a lot of young
Black consumers who would be the target of Nike ads trying to get them
to buy new styles of Nike shoes. An image of a White soccer player like
David Beckham might not be as resonant with the same target audience.
Ads usually evoke ideas and feelings that are complexly related to the surrounding social world of the target audience. The image of Michael Jordan
soaring through the air to dunk a basketball might evoke feelings of freedom
and power that are at odds with the economic reality many Black youth in
the US have to content with, for example. Rather than simply reflect or
express the culture of the audience, the image might be a way of pushing
against it by suggesting ways of transcending through fantasy and consumption what cannot be so easily attained through individual action in a
highly limiting economic environment.

Advertisements, because they are so dependent for their effectiveness on
being anchored in their cultural moment, are interesting in part for how
they record differences or changes in consumer cultures. China was a communist society up until the late 1970s, when it began to slowly move toward
capitalism. Businesses were allowed to exist, markets to exchange goods to
come into being, and property to be owned and traded. A new consumer
culture came into being that included advertisements. Ads of sorts existed
before, usually in the form of wall posters, but they advertised Communist
Party ideas or polemics that people engaged in. It would have been considered an affront to communist ideals to advertise something for sale for
a profit. Nevertheless, cultures that change as dramatically as China's has
also possess continuities with the past. In one advertisement for a new
housing development in Shanghai, for example, the "four basic principles

of communist ideology" become the "Four Basic Rights of Enclave Dwellers," and those are for fairly mundane things – a van pool, mail delivery, installment payments, and a green setting. But they are also daily creature comforts that make life for people easier, especially if they are the middle income people targeted by this housing development who cannot afford the taxis and drivers that more wealthy Shanghai dwellers can. The ads for housing addressed to the wealthy emphasize values such as privacy (*siren*) that would have been quite alien to Communist China just a few decades before. In the past, *siren* connoted selfishness of a kind condemned by both Confucianism and Communism. The ads promote images of abundance made possible by the new consumer economy, and as with such ads in Western capitalist countries, the images are of happy families made happy by consumer goods. The new reality of economic class difference disappears and shifts to the unacknowledged background of ongoing life in such advertising culture.

In a similar way, ads in the 1970s inverted gender practices by showing women in business suits patting handsome young men on the bottom. This form of sexual harassment had been practiced only by men. The clever inversion of the stereotype nevertheless left the idea and the possibility of sexual harassment intact as a practice. More recent advertisements with gender themes go further, as one would expect. In a recent Alka-Seltzer commercial, a man takes out a small packet of Alka-Seltzer after a meal with a young woman at a restaurant; he drops the package, which resembles a condom package. A man on a date might be expected to carry such a condom package "just in case," but to show it to his date would be considered bad form. She looks at the package and says, "What kind of girl do you think I am?" The implied statement is "How improper of you to presume we would have sex after this dinner." We then see the seltzer in water fizzing away, calming the man's now very upset stomach. And in the final image, the woman holds up a condom package and says, "Dessert?" The joke is that she is in fact "enlightened" regarding the possibility of sex with a man she is dating for the first time. And she herself initiates – an uncharacteristic gesture in a culture in which men are still largely supposed to take the lead in courtship. The ad works by inverting the stereotype it first presents as true – the idea that a young woman might or should be offended by sexual interest or presumption on the part of a male on a first date. A past cultural assumption is preserved and cited, but only in order to be comically revised and undermined.

Student Exercise

One of the most interesting controversies regarding advertisement and its social implications in recent years concerned the campaign by Dove to make girls more aware of how the beauty industry imposes an image of beauty on them that is at odds with how most girls look. Analyze the debate and write a position paper on it. Pay particular attention to how the various ads work as ads. How do they work to persuade? How do they use images, narrative, character, and so on? Finally, are the Axe body spray commercials continuous with a sexist tradition or do they invert and transform it?

Here are some important links:

http://www.youtube.com/watch?v=iYhCn0jf46U
http://www.youtube.com/watch?v=Ei6JvK0W60I&feature=related
http://www.youtube.com/watch?v=I9tWZB7OUSU&NR=1
http://www.youtube.com/watch?v=g_ySo29c-Gg&NR=1
http://www.youtube.com/watch?v=3VDsLcl72Ss&feature=PlayList
  &p=209F992D0596E67F&playnext=1&index=19
http://jezebel.com/306063/the-inconvenient-truth-behind-dove-
  the-love+your+body-beauty-company

Or you might pursue the following question:

In late 2008, Vaseline began a new advertising campaign which combined aspects of word-of-mouth and viral advertising. The Prescribe the Nation campaign was designed to promote a new product, Vaseline Clinical Therapy Lotion, described as a "prescription-strength lotion without the prescription." The campaign started in Kodiak, Alaska; one woman, Petal Ruch, was given a supply of Vaseline Clinical Therapy and asked to "prescribe" it to her friends. Vaseline was hoping to take advantage of the strong social networks which existed in Kodiak, as well obtain testimonials about the effectiveness of the lotion in even the extreme climate of Alaska. Within two weeks, almost 1,000 people in the community had been "prescribed" the lotion. Vaseline launched http://www.prescribethenation.com, where consumers could see the stories of Kodiak residents, and obtain a coupon by "prescribing" themselves or others. A site header states that as of week 20 of the campaign, 1,444,115 people have been "prescribed."[3]

The Prescribe the Nation campaign is an example of a highly successful viral campaign; however, campaigns which are based primarily upon the response of the consumer are notoriously fickle. If the consumers do not respond in the hoped-for manner, the campaign will fail or, worse, become an object of scorn. When a video appeared at alliwantforxmasisapsp.com (this site no longer exists) in 2006, featuring a young man rapping about his desire for a PSP, some viewers were skeptical. A group of posters on the Something Awful forums quickly revealed the video to be the work of a marketing agency working for Sony. This failed campaign came less than a year after Sony's widely criticized guerilla-marketing attempt to promote the PSP. This 2005 attempt hired graffiti artists to spray-paint buildings with images of kids using a PSP in fantastical ways (such as riding it like a horse), and did not feature Sony's name or logo anywhere. Neither of these campaigns was successful in increasing sales, and both created significant amounts of hostility toward the company. (The PSP video, along with some background information, can be accessed at http://www.youtube.com/watch?v=tX_3GEvF8RQ. A *New York Times* article on Sony's graffiti campaign can be accessed at http://www.nytimes.com/2005/12/12/business/media/12sony.html.)[4]

Both Vaseline and Sony attempted to tap into existing social networks that might have had a need or a desire for their respective products, with the intention that the members of these networks would promote their products. However, while Vaseline successfully utilized these networks, Sony ended up alienating themselves from the members of the social networks they were targeting. What were the similarities between the two campaigns? Why was Vaseline's campaign so successful while Sony's failed? Were there any elements present in one campaign but not the other? Is there a way that Sony could have altered either of its campaigns to make them more successful?

Notes

1. Lambesis Research Group, "The L Report®," http://www.lreport.com (accessed October 10, 2009).
2. The Cool Hunter, "The Cool Hunter: Roaming the U.S. & the Globe ... So You're in the Know," http://www.thecoolhunter.net (accessed October 10, 2009); and Marc Ecko, "Marc Ecko's Complex.com," http://www.complex.com/blogs/2009/01/06/street-detail-canadas-cool-hunter/ (accessed October 10, 2009).
3. Vaseline, "Prescribe the Nation," http://www.prescribethenation.com (accessed October 10, 2009).
4. "Sony PSP Marketing Ad: 'All I Want for Christmas Is My PSP,'" http://www.youtube.com/watch?v=tX_3GEvF8RQ (accessed October 10, 2009); and Matt Richtel, "Sony Got Hip, but the Hipsters Got Sony," *New York Times*, December 12, 2005, http://www.nytimes.com/2005/12/12/business/media/12sony.html (accessed October 10, 2009).

Sources

On fashion and clothing, see Roland Barthes, *The Fashion System* (New York, 1990); John Potvin, ed., *The Places and Spaces of Fashion* (New York, 2009); Caroline Evans, *Fashion at the Edge: Spectacle, Modernity, and Deathliness* (New Haven, Conn., 2003); Diana Crane, *Fashion and Its Social Agendas: Class, Gender, and Identity in Clothing* (Chicago, 2000); and Fred Davis, *Fashion, Culture, and Identity* (Chicago, 1994).

9

Music

with Brett Ingram

When we talk about films, television shows, books, or politics, we often ask if they "make sense": whether or not they fulfill our expectations of what is reasonable, likely, or possible based on what we know of how life works. We measure these things according to a standard of realism – how much they approximate or accurately represent the world as we know it, our reality. When we discuss music, on the other hand, we tend to use impressionistic language that refers to experiences of sight (Goth music is "dark"), smell (blues music is "funky"), taste (sentimental ballads are "saccharine"), or touch (rock is either "hard" or "soft"). We may still question if music "makes sense," but our use of the term draws our attention more directly to what it makes us feel and what it makes our bodies do, rather than what it makes us think. At its best, music seems to circumvent rational thought and transport us to a realm of sensual, pre-verbal existence. Our reaction is almost primal, or spiritual, and the conventional wisdom suggests that to think too much about music is to rob it of some of its pleasure. As the Eminem song suggests, you have to "lose yourself in the music" in order to achieve this state of transcendence. This is a theme echoed in many pop lyrics. In her 1980s hit "Get into The Groove," Madonna encourages the listener to do that very thing, and to "let the music set you free"; AC/DC's classic "For Those About to Rock (We Salute You)" turns the name of a genre into a verb, as does Justin Timberlake's single "Rock Your Body," something he proposes doing "until the break of day." In all of these examples, and in many other pop songs, the words that accompany the music point self-referentially back to the sensory experience of embodiment, affect, and immediacy rather than to some external reality of clearly defined people, places, and things that the music represents or seeks to approximate. Music occupies a vaguely defined territory which blurs the distinction between mind and body, conscious and unconscious experience, the self and others. This makes it a particularly tricky, but also richly rewarding, subject for serious study.

You may have noticed it's a bit awkward, even comical, to consider lyrics in written form, or to ask things such as "What is a 'groove,' exactly, and how do I go about getting into one? If a groove sets me free, what is otherwise holding me down? What can I find by losing myself in the music? What is the definition of 'to rock'?" The answer to all these questions may be that if you have to ask, you just don't get it.

Explicating lyrics is such a strange endeavor because in most cases, they aren't supposed to be read out of context. The message, the sound, and the contextual experience of listening are tightly bound together. People who study popular music take it as their task to pry apart the many different layers of social energies and power relations that combine to make music a universally meaningful phenomenon, and to hold each of these elements up to the light of critical scrutiny. Some such as Lawrence Grossberg attend to music's affective aspects, its ability to record and create feeling states as well as to foster "affective alliances" between like-feeling people in music subcultures. Others such as Adam Krims attend more to the structure, form, and content of the music, as if it were a static object or aesthetic product considered apart from its lived immediacy or its affective experience.

If we are to comprehend the values, anxieties, and desires of a particular culture, we must understand the practices that surround the production and consumption of its music. It is often assumed that scholars are only interested in important historical events like wars, stock market crashes, and elections. However, great social movements do not occur in a sphere removed from artistic and cultural life, which includes popular entertainments like music. Rather, these things are mutually determined and determining; in other words, changes in political and economic institutions create changes in art and music, and vice versa. A rock 'n' roll song may not be enough to start a political overthrow, but it can help set forces into motion which eventually coalesce into revolutionary struggle. Similarly, corruption in the government may seem far removed from a dingy rock club or an urban block party, but it is the pervasive mood of distrust and defiance engendered by cynical abuses of power that inspires musicians to pick up instruments, plug in turntables, and create the art that moves the masses.

Of course, not all popular music acts as a catalyst for social change. Indeed, most of it is more concerned with dancing and partying than it is with protest marches and Molotov cocktails. Pop music's aspirations are often directed toward producing interpersonal enjoyment rather than political awareness, and our interactions with music are in many cases extensions of our leisure time interactions with other human beings, something we may think of as separate from political and public affairs. This should not diminish music's relevance as a subject of critical reflection, for music's ubiquity in the most intimate aspects of our personal lives heightens its power to mold us as both private individuals and public citizens. Our attitudes toward major social issues are conditioned by the emotional reactions we have to encounter in our everyday lives, and very few of those encounters occur without music. Put another way, the personal is political. Ask yourself: in the first decade of the twenty-first century, who has more direct impact on the way an average American teenager constructs her ideas about what it means to be a "good" or "attractive" girl – Hillary Clinton or Britney Spears? Whose attitudes do most adolescent males adopt when faced with bewildering encounters with a member of the opposite sex – Pope Benedict XVI or Kanye West? Whose poetry has captured the imagination of more young people – John Ashbery or Tupac Shakur? Common sense tells us that popular music has a role in shaping the worldviews of young people which eclipses that of traditional authority figures. Our subjective conceptions of self-worth, sexual difference, social justice, and artistic merit have a direct effect on how we'll vote, how we'll raise our children, what we'll buy, and what we will fight and perhaps even die for.

Moreover, music foregrounds pleasure and the pleasurable experience of one's body in motion on a dance floor. Perhaps for this reason it has often been attacked by moral monitors who feel that pleasure should be policed and that bodily experiences should be restrained because they are connected to sexuality, which of course itself, from a conservative perspective, should be controlled as much as possible. One of funnier moments in the film *The Full Monty* depicts a Black man standing in line at an employment agency idly and un-self-consciously moving his body rhythmically to the music of a dance number he is practicing that is running through his mind. He is breaking the conventions of how one is normally supposed to stand in line – rigidly, motionless, and without joy or other affect. He is joyfully waiting rather than waiting. Much of our experience in a disciplined society that assigns proper places to certain activities and forbids them in others is limited and limiting. We unconsciously play by rules of motion and bodily experience that channel and determine what we can or cannot do in certain places. Music challenges those rules by creating pleasure and diffusing it across social boundaries – a tendency made more emphatic by digital music players. A capitalist society especially demands that we work in a disciplined fashion for others for their profit (the motto of the society being "Never have so many worked so hard so that so few could enjoy themselves so much"), but music gives everyone access to a certain degree of pleasure even if they are not on the wealth-magnet end of the social pyramid.

Think of all the different ways you encounter music in your daily life. You may be jarred awake by a radio alarm clock playing a roaring metal song; transform your walk through campus from a mundane ritual to a cinematic adventure by selecting a soundtrack from your iPod; notice a barely perceptible romantic ballad staving off uncomfortable silence as you shop at the supermarket; flip on the television and see Bruce Springsteen's anti-war protest song "Born in the USA" being played at a political rally celebrating America's latest military action; go to a college party, where people writhe to hip hop songs about the brutality of street life; and ease your way into sleep with some ambient music by Brian Eno. In the latter part of the twentieth century, music evolved from being something people consciously chose to experience in clearly defined contexts such as concerts, dances, or ceremonial events to something that pervades nearly our every waking moment, and influences at an almost subliminal level our emotional responses to the phenomena with which we're confronted in all aspects of our daily lives. Music makes arguments without seeming to do so. Or, more accurately, human agents use music to persuade us to think and act in particular ways. There is purpose and design behind the music we hear in offices, in stores, on commercials, and at social gatherings. It is intended to send a message: "Get to work," "Buy this," or "You are one of us." When analyzing music's social function, we must always remember that no use or production of music is arbitrary or accidental, and that all engagements with music have effects that resonate beyond the fleeting moment of the listening encounter.

For instance, music is one of the primary ways by which we create and maintain our identities, our sense of who we are and how we fit into the world. We often choose to associate with other people based on shared tastes in particular musical performers or genres and the ideologies they represent. The formation of individual and group identities around music is often a source of apprehension, and sometimes hysteria, among authority figures. This unease is particularly intense when a new style of music, along with new ways for music fans to dress and behave, supplants the previous generation's preferred musical aesthetic. When jazz burst into the American popular consciousness in the 1940s, it was derided by the White establishment as the work of sexual deviants and drug abusers, personified by the shiftless beatnik; the same criticism was leveled at rock 'n' roll in the 1950s (greasers), acid rock in the 1960s (hippies), heavy metal in the 1970s (stoners), and, most recently, hip hop (gangstas). The public moral panics which so often attend the emergence of new forms of popular music all share a concern that young people will be induced to act in socially destructive or self-destructive ways by music that subdues the listener's conscience with its hypnotic beats and rhythms. Because it is sensual rather than sensible, music presents new possibilities for the body which are at odds with prevailing normative codes of responsible social conduct centered on work and duty. New forms of music are considered dangerous because they lead ostensibly impressionable listeners to question the logic and inevitability of value systems which insist that the body must properly be used for labor and reproduction rather than pleasure and self-expression.

Since the dawn of Western civilization, music has been a source of profound anxiety because of its ability to inspire subversive thought and action. The ancient Greeks attributed to music the capacity to strengthen or degrade people's character. They went so far as to assign different moral values to each musical scale, so that some tones were believed to cause aggression and violence, while others encouraged noble conduct. Plato posited a correlation between the movements of the soul and the rhythms of music. He maintained that music was not a superficial means of amusement, but rather, a key component in education, the aim of which was to achieve self-mastery over the passions and strengthen moral character. Thus, music was not a private matter, but a public one. The cultivation of "good" music led to a more ordered soul in the listener, and therefore a more ethical and disciplined citizenry, whereas "bad" music dangerously enflamed individual passions, and thus fostered discord in the community. Plato claimed that "the introduction of a new kind of music must be shunned as imperiling the whole state; since styles of music are never disturbed without affecting the most important political institutions." While Plato wrote this in 360 BC, his basic premise still resonates in the contemporary world. We may perceive traces of it in widespread beliefs that hip hop music, rather than outrage over police brutality and systemic racism, compels young men to commit acts of violence against law enforcement officers, or that the music of Marilyn Manson, rather than skepticism toward a scandal-ridden religious establishment, turns young people away from traditional Christian values.

As we can see, guardians of public morality have always taken seriously music's capacity to affect the minds and bodies of listeners, and the moral values they so vigorously defend can usually be defined as those attitudes and behaviors which prove beneficial to the dominant group's efforts to maintain and solidify their social and economic power. In America, the dominant group is predominantly White, male, middle class, heterosexual, and Christian, and it has historically been resistant to adopting, or even tolerating, value systems and lifestyles that do not fit within that paradigm. However, it has been eager to enthusiastically consume the artistic products of marginalized cultures, and to incorporate these products into its own cultural tradition. For instance, disco, a mainstream national phenomenon in the 1970s, was sonically rooted in Black funk and R&B, and indebted to the gay club scene for its visual aesthetic. The rhythmic beat, emotional energy, and sexual frankness that characterize rock 'n' roll are elements taken from African American blues music, which itself developed out of the traditional African music brought to the New World by slavery. The history of American popular music is consistently one of White artists' appropriations of Black cultural forms as a means of attaining prominence and profit. While White artists such as Elvis Presley, the Beatles, and Bob Dylan are often given credit for originating the rock 'n' roll sound, they were most significantly influenced by Black rhythm and blues musicians who have become footnotes to music history. This is a matter of considerable tension among Black artists; as Public Enemy's Chuck D. declared in the seminal, incendiary single "Fight the Power," "Elvis was a hero to most / but he never meant shit to me." Many artists and critics argue that musical styles represent more than just formulaic arrangement of sounds; they are ways to mark territory, to carve out a space of ownership and exclusivity in a world increasingly marked by the free flow of images and ideas across cultural and regional boundaries.

The expansions of global capitalism and developments in media technology have dramatically increased most people's access to different kinds of music. With a few clicks of a button, you can download music from the other side of the earth, share it with your friends, and remix it to suit your purposes. What is gained is a greater sense and appreciation of the diversity of musical expression; what is sometimes lost is a full understanding of the social conditions and contexts from which that music is produced.

One result of this is a media environment in which we no longer raise an eyebrow when Janis Joplin's "Mercedes Benz," a mournful indictment of materialism, is featured in a commercial for the luxury car manufacturer, or "Lust for Life," Iggy Pop's ode to drug culture, is used to promote wholesome Royal Caribbean cruises. On the other hand, the practice of sampling – lifting a segment of recorded music from its original source and incorporating it into a new song – is a keystone of much contemporary dance and hip hop music, and has enabled the creation of exciting new musical compositions fashioned from a bricolage of borrowed sounds. Sampling has sparked lawsuits by individuals and corporations who own copyrights to songs and believe they should be paid whenever those songs are used to make profit for others. However, many artists maintain that sampling is essentially no different from White rock 'n' roll artists' appropriation of rhythm and blues, soul, and gospel, the intellectual property rights of which are rarely discussed in public or legal discourse.

Due in large part to advances in media technology, in recent decades delineations between musical genres, and between the subcultures that grow around them, have become more permeable, and new hybrid forms are beginning to appear. Successful mainstream artists such as the Rage against the Machine and Linkin Park blend rap and hard rock; Missy Elliot and M.I.A merge hip hop with Southeast Asian instrumental arrangements; Shakira and Jennifer Lopez inject Hispanic influences into dance music. Given the fluidity with which contemporary artists and fans move between genres and musical traditions, it may seem unbelievable that young men from the same socioeconomic class once engaged in physical combat over differences in musical tastes, as British "mods" and "rockers" did in the early 1960s. Of course, it would be inaccurate to claim that the hybridization of musical genres signals the end of tensions between identity groups. Instead, we must consider the ways in which the lines that divide people according to differences in race, ethnicity, gender, sexuality, and social class are continually being redrawn, and the ways in which music both challenges and reaffirms those divisions.

The cross-pollination of musical sounds and themes occurs not only across genres in the American music scene, but is increasingly a transnational phenomenon. Indeed, it is problematic to speak of *American* or *Middle Eastern* or *South American* music as separate and distinct categories anymore. In the American recording industry, the term *world music* is used to market music made by indigenous people that is strongly informed by their native traditions. Many critics argue that this designation reinforces the false idea that non-Western or rural music emanates from exotic civilizations "untainted" by modern Western influence. As a result, world music is often regarded as unsophisticated and obscure, and thought to be decipherable only to savvy connoisseurs. However, much contemporary non-Western music is a dynamic mix of local and international styles, and is neither strictly beholden to a romanticized, more "authentic" past, nor a diluted imitation of popular American genres. It represents a reality in which, for better or worse, no region on earth is immune to the effects of globalization and modernity. The dichotomy between world music and Western popular music perpetuated by marketing categories is actually a simplification of a much more complicated and interesting story.

Let's take for illustration the case of Palestinian hip hop. The Palestine territories, fiercely disputed lands which lie within the region captured by Israel in 1967, are to a large degree ruled by Hamas, the Islamic Resistance Movement, which advocates the destruction of the State of Israel and the establishment of a Palestinian Islamic state in its wake. In strict accord with Islamic fundamentalist principles, Hamas considers secular music to be a potentially blasphemous practice and therefore *haram* ("forbidden"). It especially disapproves of music that is accompanied by suggestive movement, that encourages the mixing of men and women, or that seeks to arouse the sexual drives. Public performances of such music are often met with angry mobs of Hamas supporters firing machine guns and hurling stones. This may not seem like a context from which hip hop could flourish, and yet, there are a number of Palestinian musicians who adopt the oppositional attitude and heavy beats of American hip hop to express resistance to Israeli occupation, Hamas oppression, and Western imperialism.

The first and perhaps most prominent Palestinian rappers, DAM (Da Arabian MCs), combine the Arabic language, Middle Eastern melodies, and urban American hip hop to create a compelling hybrid sound. They acknowledge their indebtedness to American rap while also staking a claim to a unique and independent space within their own culture in witty and provocative rhymes, such as this verse from "Hibuna Istruna" ("Love Us and Buy Us"):

> Who was your influence?' – I'll tell you who
> I'm like Sinbad, I'll reach every land
> With my flying carpet the mic, I'll open every secret door
> "How do you know the password?" well, I grew up an Ali Baba
> And using foreign tradition I'm bringing us back to our tradition.

Ali Baba is a character in the ancient Arabian story collection *One Thousand and One Nights* who eavesdrops on a group of thieves and uses what he's heard to unlock a magic cave containing stolen treasure. DAM ground their appropriation of hip hop in the imagery and folklore of their native culture. DAM, like Ali Baba, listens in to the discourse of "outsiders" – in this case, American rappers – then uses the knowledge gained to "open doors," that is, to make their voices heard in a society that denies its citizens freedom of expression.

The title "Love Us and Buy Us" must be read ironically, as the song is a critique of the hedonism and materialism which have come to dominate much contemporary American hip hop music. For example, DAM asks,

> Wanna shake? Go ahead and shake your head to expel your thoughts
> But if you only shake your ass all you'll do is expel shit
> Ohhh is it forbidden to say that? I can't say it?
> You can't say "you can't" in hip hop music, it's free
> Now check it out.

DAM seek to establish middle territory between the polarized positions of Islamic extremists who reject hip hop's decadence and immorality on religious grounds, and hip hop aficionados who celebrate decadence and immorality for its own sake. Shaking the head – a gesture of pious negativity – is likened to thoughtlessness, while shaking the posterior – a gesture of impious carnality – is presented as equally unproductive. DAM suggest that secular Western civilization is debased by its addiction to the pleasures of the flesh, fundamentalist Islamic culture is misguided by its obsession with the sanctity of the spirit, and that thoughtful moderation is the best alternative. "Moderation" is not a theme we'll find very often in American hip hop, but as we can see, the genre is adaptable to contexts that extend far beyond its country of origin.

You may have noticed the preponderance of geographical metaphors in this chapter, words like space, lines, territory, boundaries, and grounds. Popular music is a tool people who lack adequate physical or symbolic space in society can use to make their presence and needs known. Sometimes this takes the form of name-checking specific places or regions in songs, such as references in rap to *Eastside* or *Westside*, which denote New York or Los Angeles affiliations. In other cases, it is a matter of foregrounding a distinguishing regional characteristic, such as the thick Southern drawl employed by Toby Keith, or Wyclef Jean's tendency to intermittently punctuate his vocal delivery with Haitian patois. These techniques are more than just stylistic devices; they force into the public consciousness voices and perspectives that are otherwise rarely acknowledged. To use another spatial image, popular music has always been the preferred expressive medium of "outsiders." This can mean teenagers alienated from the parent generation, ethnic minorities thrust to the margins of society by racial prejudice, class-based collectives who feel disenfranchised by diminished economic opportunities, or any other group that feels distanced from the dominant way of life in a particular sociohistorical context. In business or politics, being an outsider is often an impediment to power, but in popular music, it tends to be a desirable sign of authenticity which grants access to the spotlight to those who usually go unnoticed, and makes others want to listen, learn, and act. Pop music is one of the few cultural arenas where the poor and the dispossessed enjoy a rare place of privilege.

However, we must not paint a too rosy picture of pop music's egalitarian spirit. The double-edged sword of an outsider, oppositional art is that, by definition, it must exclude in order maintain its self-definition as a separate entity, apart from that which it opposes – for there to be an "us," there has to be a "them." Unfortunately, the divisions which arise within popular music sometimes mimic the inequities and injustices of the wider society. Hip hop is infected by virulent homophobia, country music is frequently jingoistic and xenophobic, and nearly ever popular genre is to some degree marred by sexism. We may consider, for instance, the vexed position of women in rock 'n' roll. The music industry has traditionally been a microcosm of the larger patriarchal social order. Men held the economic power as the major players in the recording industry, they wielded creative control as producers and songwriters, and more often than not, they sang the songs and played the instruments. Women were usually relegated to the role of fans, backup singers, or objects of heterosexual desire in lyrics. When they did appear front and center onstage or on television, they were framed as coy temptresses whose only desire was for romantic love. In the 1950s women were not allowed to join the Musician's Union, and in the 1960s, most "girl groups" had names that ended in "-ette" or "-elle" (e.g., the Ronettes, the Chantels, the Shirelles), suggesting they were a diminutive imitation of more legitimate male groups. While female rock musicians in the late 1960s and 1970s such as Janis Joplin, Patti Smith, and Debbie Harry enjoyed commercial success operating in the male-dominated mode of electric guitar rock, critical evaluations of their work tend to foreground their gender in a way male artists rarely experience – we don't find special issues of music magazines or documentaries dedicated to "Men in Rock" – and these women are often back-handedly praised for their ability to be "one of the boys," that is, to display the lust and swagger usually coded as masculine.

In the 1980s and 1990s, pop stars such as Madonna and Gwen Stefani toyed self-consciously with sexist stereotypes, while other female artists, Alanis Morissette and Courtney Love among them, embraced the aggressive dynamic of hard rock and combined it with raw, confessional lyrics that expressed a greater emotional complexity than has normally been permitted of women in the genre. And yet, it is questionable whether women in mainstream music have achieved the level of artistic freedom accorded to male pop musicians, who are regularly able to experiment with gender-bending aesthetics and a varied palette of lyrical themes without fear of being pigeonholed or censured. While women's creative control over their images and artistic output has increased substantially in recent years, most female artists must still trade upon their sexuality to some degree in order to achieve recognition in the mainstream music media.

A review of the brief but tumultuous career of Britney Spears may help illuminate the ways in which music culture rewards or punishes female artists based upon their adherence to or rejection of narrowly defined categories of acceptable performances of sexuality. Spears' breakout 1998 single "Baby One More Time" was immensely successful, topping the charts for two weeks and helping her debut album sell more than 25 million copies worldwide. What garnered more attention than the song itself was the public persona that was crafted for her. The 17-year-old singer embodied a titillating confluence of womanly sexual sophistication and girlish innocence. She appeared on the cover of *Rolling Stone* wearing a push-up bra and cradling a child's doll, danced provocatively in a Lolitaesque schoolgirl outfit in her video, and publicly pledged to abstain from sex until marriage. Spears was strategically situated in two ideals of femininity that are usually diametrically opposed: she was both virgin and whore, an illicit temptress who covered the tracks of her transgression with a sweetly naïve cover story. She was simultaneously the nubile sexual object that heterosexual males could leer at, the sexually empowered teen-ager that adolescent girls could aspire to be, and the polite, Southern

Christian daughter that mothers could approve of. However, as Spears grew up and it became clear that she was a sexually active adult (stories of erotic liaisons with rock stars and young actors filled the tabloids), and as her music and performances became more openly sexual (a televised awards show appearance saw her dancing lewdly with a giant snake while singing "I'm a Slave 4 U"), public opinion turned against her, and she became the subject of almost universal scorn and mockery. It is noteworthy that the attacks leveled against her were framed in the discourses of class (she was "White trash") and psychiatry (she was a nymphomaniac or simply insane). This is remarkably similar to Victorian-era conceptions of sexuality, in which pronounced female desire was linked to either "low" class status or biological abnormality.

In general, mainstream American music consumers demand that female artists announce their sexual role and stick with it. They will accept the performance of forthright sexual promiscuity (Christina Aguilera, Madonna) or sexual modesty (Mandy Moore, Jessica Simpson), but when female artists dare to evolve into sexual maturity with all of its contradictions and complexities, they are disciplined with decreased record sales and public disparagement. For contrast, consider the career trajectory of Justin Timberlake who, like Spears, started out as a chaste teenage performer, but who has developed into an adult artist whose music is at times openly lascivious, and at other times sappily romantic. Music fans and critics neither perceived dissonance in his steady transformation from boy to man, nor expressed hostility to work that moves erratically between the yearning for love and the demand for sex. This is testament to significant differences in the range of identities made available to men and women both in music and in society at large.

While this analysis of sexual performance and gender in pop music suggests a conservative undercurrent that flows beneath what is in many other respects a very progressive art form, it must be noted that a number of successful mainstream female artists, and many more operating in underground music subcultures, are currently testing the limits of what Americans will tolerate in terms of sexual provocation and fluidity in gender role behavior. Careful attention to popular music gives us a good sense of where the culture is at and what direction it is headed next. Pop music is sometimes derided for its disposability, the rapidity with which faddish bands and sounds come and go, but a correlate to this is the constant necessity for renewal which sends artists and fans in a perpetual hunt for innovative ideas and fresh sounds. Perhaps more than any other cultural practice, it is predicated on changes – rhythmic, stylistic, and ideological – which compel the bodies and minds of listeners to move in ways they hadn't before thought possible.

The development of new forms of music is more a matter of evolution than of invention, insofar as individual artists invariably build upon and borrow from that which came before them. Musicians refashion styles and themes from other cultural traditions in order to comment upon, and in some cases intervene in, the social relations of their own specific contexts. Popular music often addresses the limitations and injustices inherent in the hierarchical categorization of people in terms of race, ethnicity, class, gender, and sexuality. It has the ability to destabilize seemingly "fixed" social roles, and to redistribute cultural power to marginalized and oppressed groups.

Let's take a look at the way one influential and controversial artist, Eminem, uses his music to interrogate the logic behind divisions of race and class in contemporary America. One of the central debates surrounding Eminem involves his appropriation of a traditionally Black music, hip hop, to tell the story of his experience growing up in the White working class. Some Black critics argue that Eminem, like Elvis Presley or Vanilla Ice before him, reaps the rewards granted for performing Black music without experiencing the racism that comprises the backdrop of the Black music tradition – "everything but the burden," as scholar Greg Tate puts it. But Eminem complicates the issue, for he was raised in the impoverished working-class neighborhoods of Detroit, a product of the same economic conditions that produced most Black rap artists.

Eminem represents a social group that is both visible and invisible in mainstream culture: "White trash." We routinely see mocking references to White trash in comedy routines, commercials, movies, and television shows, yet there are very few thoughtful portrayals of what it is actually like to live as a person who inhabits a racially privileged body, but who lacks the economic power that is often assumed to "naturally" go along with Whiteness. It often goes unnoticed that the negative qualities attributed to White trash are very similar to the racist tropes directed at African Americans: both are marked by stereotypes of sexual excess, poverty, danger, laziness, and non-normative family structures. While White trash is banished to the margins within the dominant culture, and racial minorities are relegated to the margins outside of the dominant culture, the experience of both groups is one of alienation from mainstream society, which is most often represented as White and middle class. Eminem's use of Black music to articulate the suffering of impoverished Whites disrupts widely held racial and class assumptions by drawing explicit parallels between the lived conditions of working-class Whites and Blacks, and by challenging the myth that Whiteness is synonymous with economic privilege. Eminem neither attempts to "be Black" nor celebrates "White trashness" – in fact, he is quite critical of the prejudices held by some members of the White working class. The argument he makes through his music is nuanced: he claims that living at the bottom of the economic scale is a miserable existence for anyone, regardless of skin color, and that hip hop "authenticity" is based in neither race nor class, but more generally in the experience of deprivation and the desire for a better life.

We can examine how music functions in one scene from *8 Mile*, the 2002 biographical film that spawned a chart-topping album of the same name, to get a sense of Eminem's careful strategy for negotiating delicate issues of race and class. Immediately preceding the scene we'll consider, Eminem's character, Rabbit, has been publicly humiliated in a hip hop battle competition at a local nightclub when he is unable to respond to lyrical assault from a Black rapper who uses Rabbit's Whiteness as the theme of his attack. Compounding this, Rabbit returns home to the trailer park to find his unemployed mother having sex in the living room with her drunken, similarly unemployed boyfriend. As a gesture of conciliation, and a poor attempt at a birthday present, she gives him the keys to her rusted, broken-down old sedan, which Rabbit and his Black friend Future attempt to repair the next morning. As the two men work on the car, strains of Lynyrd Skynyrd's "Sweet Home Alabama" issue forth from the trailer, accompanied by Rabbit's mother's boyfriend's – Greg Buell's – drunken attempts to sing along. Greg is visually characterized as the White trash archetype, clad in a Ford T-shirt and ripped jeans, a cigarette protruding from his unshaven face. His taste in music is suggestive of his worldviews. Lynyrd Skynyrd were champions of working-class, Southern White culture (which is commonly aligned with White trash), and often played stage shows with a Confederate flag as a backdrop. The song "Sweet Home Alabama" has a notorious association with bigotry. The lines "I hope Neil Young will remember / a Southern man don't need him around, anyhow" are a response to Neil Young's anti-racist song "Southern Man," which featured the lyrics,

I saw cotton
I saw black
Tall white mansions and little shacks
Southern man
when will you pay them back?
I heard screamin'
and bullwhips cracking
How long? How long?

Furthermore, "Sweet Home Alabama" contains the verse, "Now in Birmingham they love the Governor," which refers to segregationist Alabama Governor George Wallace. By aligning Greg Buell's working-class Whiteness with a taste for what is considered by many to be racist music, *8 Mile* conflates racism with class, and in so doing provides Eminem with a cultural milieu from which he can righteously seek to escape. The idea of escape from racism, prejudice, and poverty, an overarching theme in rap music, is skillfully transplanted intact onto a racial identity traditionally viewed within the genre as that of the oppressor. Rather than cynically appropriating Black working-class suffering, Eminem makes the case that escaping from within the territory of the oppressor makes him empathetic with, and equal to, the condition of the oppressed. Simply put, he argues it is possible to be an Other within White working-class culture, to feel oppressed by your own people, even if you are yourself White and working class.

Having symbolically positioned himself on the side of the oppressed Other, Eminem performs an act common to Others: he appropriates the music of the oppressor to articulate his dissatisfaction, free-styling rap lyrics over "Sweet Home Alabama." He mockingly assumes the exaggerated southern twang associated with White trash, and speaks of trailer park reality rather than urban ghetto life: "Now I'm living at home in trailer/ What the hell am I supposed to do?" In a show of unity, Future adds his own commentary on Rabbit's situation: "Well Jimmy [Rabbit's real name] moved in with his mother/'Cause he ain't got no place to go," and Rabbit continues the verse, "Now I'm right back in the gutter/with a garbage bag that's full of clothes." At the conclusion of the scene, Future reveals that he has signed Rabbit up for another rap battle, and pleads to his reluctant friend to participate, arguing that his skills will redeem him, and the matter of race will be forgotten: "Once they hear you, it won't matter what color you are!" Rather than trying to force his way into a resistant Black artistic community, the White rapper in *8 Mile* is actually invited, indeed begged, to add his voice to hip hop discourse.

Student Exercise

Anyone who doubts popular music is connected to bodily life has only to watch someone listening to an iPod and swaying to the beat to see the connection. Youth popular music especially is associated with motion, energy, and bodily desire. At this point in life, sexuality especially is freshest and newest, a field of exploration that opens multiple possible routes of connection to others. Emotions are tightly wound with sexuality, and the successes and failures of connection that sexual desire produces register in emotional chords of many notes, both high and low. Youth culture in general and youth music culture especially is a zone where old conventions are almost by necessity challenged and rethought. The last thing most new generations want to do is to live by the rules of the old. Those challenges and explorations make popular youth music one of the most interesting sites for understanding culture as creation and exploration, the remaking of culture understood as the architecture of our lives that maintains stability.

Consider two Katy Perry songs, "Hot N Cold" and "I Kissed a Girl." Look at the videos on YouTube.[1] "Hot N Cold" poses an immediate challenge to older gender forms. The girl bride is the primary active agent; the boy is passive, the one being chased. Until recently, men were expected to be the primary agents of romantic pursuit. But notice how the song evokes and preserves those older forms. The girl bride treats the man as if he were a "girl" and even compares his vacillation about love and commitment to that of a girl choosing clothes and not being able to decide what to wear. So the song, while challenging stereotypes and conventions, also evokes them and would even seem to endorse them. Is it both radical and conservative at once?

Discuss "I Kissed a Girl" in these same terms. Where are implied cultural norms and rules present in the song and the video? How does the song challenge them? Does it nevertheless endorse and preserve them? Compare it with Jill Sobule's song of the same name (available at http://www.youtube.com/watch?v=k4r41vPTF8k&feat ure=PlayList&p=8421B1E229EEDAA2&playnext=1&playnext_ from=PL&index=9).[2]

Notes

1. Katy Perry, "Hot N Cold," http://www.youtube.com/watch?v=9lkaf9PdlNM& feature=fvst (accessed October 8, 2009); and Katy Perry, "I Kissed a Girl," http://www.youtube.com/watch?v=kY9S3h9o9FM (accessed October 8, 2009).
2. Jill Sobule, "I Kissed a Girl" (1995), http://www.youtube.com/watch?v=k4r41v PTF8k&feature=PlayList&p=8421B1E229EEDAA2&playnext=1&playnext_ from=PL&index=9 (accessed October 8, 2009).

Sources

Joseph Kortaba, *Understanding Society through Popular Music* (New York, 2009); Carrie Havranek, *Women Icons of Popular Culture: The Rebels, Rockers, and Renegades* (Westport, Conn., 2009); Roy Shuker, *Understanding Popular Music Culture* (New York, 2008); Carolyn Stevens, *Japanese Popular Music* (New York, 2008); Hugh Barker, *Faking It: The Quest for Authenticity in Popular Music* (New York, 2007); Brian Longhurst, *Popular Music and Society* (Cambridge, UK, 2007); Simon Frith, ed,. *Taking Popular Music Seriously* (Aldershot, UK, 2007); Andy Bennett, Barry Shank, and Jason Toynbee, eds., *The Popular Music Studies Reader* (New York, 2006); Tricia Rose, *The Hip Hop Wars* (New York, 2008); Jeffrey Ogbar, *Hip-Hop Revolution* (Lawrence, Kans., 2007); Ian Condry, *Hip-Hop Japan* (Durham, N.C., 2006); and David Brackett, *The Pop, Rock, and Soul Reader* (New York, 2009).

10

Media Studies

Communication is essential to human life, and what we call *media* are essential to communication. The tongue was the first medium of communication, along with hands for making gestures. The first great communicators, who also happened to be the first great political and cultural leaders, were orators, and one of them, Cicero, a Roman legislator and lawyer, was so good at the use of his hands in oratory that when he was murdered by his enemies, they severed his hands and nailed them – along with his tongue – to the door of the Roman Senate. That horrible detail from history suggests emphatically how influential the media can be. The Romans so feared the media used by orators to sway the masses that they killed those who used them too well. The Roman Empire would not have worked without effective means of communication – papyrus and wax plates for writing, as well as a well-developed language to facilitate the communication of ideas and information and to assist the attainment of ends by influencing others to think and act in certain ways. Cicero's death was initiated using a simple medium – a posted list of Roman citizens who had been *proscribed* – literally, "written off." A proscribed citizen had ceased to have the protection of the law. He could be murdered by anyone, and his property seized by the murderer. The posted proscription list was a simple communicative medium with fatal implications. It meant life or death, and it did so by placing words in people's minds that carried ideas that initiated actions. Words work, and sometimes they work by changing the world. With Cicero's death, the era of the Roman Republic ended, and from that point forward, Rome would be ruled by emperors.

Wall posters continued to be used down through the centuries to influence public thought and behavior. In China, when it was ruled by Mao Tse-Tung's Communist Party, posters began to appear in 1963 all over Beijing. Ostensibly, posted by ordinary people, their appearance in fact

launched a campaign by Mao to regain control of the party from pragma-
tists who favored capitalist style economic development over state run
collectivism. The posters vilified his adversaries, and soon a movement
called the Cultural Revolution began that set back China's economic development and resulted in many deaths through purges. A more genuinely
popular use of posters to attain political ends occurred in Argentina in the
1980s after a repressive conservative military dictatorship finally ended.
It had suppressed a leftist movement through torture and murder, and the
mothers of those killed protested in the Plaza de Mayo, a public square,
using posters and placards that contained pictures of those who had
"disappeared." They eventually succeeded in drawing attention to the
atrocity and getting redress.

Why are the media – everything from wall posters to Internet sites – so
powerful? It is largely because they use words and images to convey ideas
that inspire action. The action they inspire can be mild and can take the
form of simple belief in something. Many people who regularly attend
action adventure movies actually believe that the images of Arabs in such
films are accurate representations of Arab reality. Or it can be extreme and
take the form of murder. When the leaders of the genocide in Rwanda in
1994 wanted to "get the word out" about what they intended to do, they
used the national radio system to broadcast calls for ethnic massacre to
begin. Or it can be both belief and action in a causal sequence. Images of
Jews propagated in German culture widely before World War II were in
part responsible for the genocide against them during the war. The images
made it possible to believe that Jews were worth killing because they posed
a threat to everything Germany's conservative leaders wanted the nation
to stand for.

But for the most part, the media are educational and rhetorical; they
shape what we think and feel; they influence us to see things in certain ways
such that our behavior in regard to them takes certain forms. They paint
the particular picture of reality we hold in our minds, and that plays an
important role in determining the choices we make as we live each day, the
beliefs and values we hold, and the things we do in the real world. That
explains why many people are so concerned about who owns the media
and why governments sometimes place limits on how much of a single
medium such as television or how many different kinds of media any one
person can own. The assumption guiding such policies is that one person
can imprint his or her way of seeing the world on the media and use them
to foster that particular picture of reality in people's minds. And if people's

action in the world – regarding everything from which political party they will vote for to whether or not they will support a war – depend on what picture of the world is in their minds, then ownership of the media and limitations on it are important issues indeed. For example, when Rupert Murdoch, a conservative known for inserting his beliefs into his news companies such as Fox News so that news reporting often seems biased toward right-wing perspectives and values, wanted to purchase the *Wall Street Journal*, a business newspaper, many feared that he would also turn that into a vehicle for his views. He was obliged to promise to refrain from doing so in order to convince the owners to sell to him.

Simply inserting a right-wing idea into a news broadcast is not likely to convince the audience to adopt it, but if the news media routinely, consistently, and repeatedly rely on one perspective or one way of depicting the world they portray and rely on, then it becomes more likely that those routinely watching and listening will be influenced in their beliefs and perceptions by it. They will "see" the world in a particular, quite limited way. In order to understand how that might be the case, you need to think about news reporting as something more than an alignment of words with facts, and you need to think of how you perceive the world as being itself a kind of picture that is painted for you by your culture and that is very different from the facts of the world.

There is a strong tendency in any culture to think of everyday reality as normal, as being as it should be. I'm always struck, living in Philadelphia, an American city with a sharp geographic division between a poor area populated by African Americans and Hispanics and a well-to-do area populated by Whites, with how strange it seems to live with such a sharp economic divide "as if" it were normal. To live in such a world sanely, the picture of it in your mind must be one that endorses it. Such pictures are linked to keywords we use to categorize the reality before us in our minds. So we use words like *poverty*, for example, for a reality such as the one around my university in Philadelphia. If we used a different set of words – such as *economic concentration camp* or *capitalist apartheid* – we might be tempted to think quite differently about that reality.

The news media foster and maintain supposedly "normal" pictures of reality in our minds by using certain words and images to represent that reality to us. Those words and images are often your only access to that reality. In a way, when you try to picture that world in your mind, what you see is the images the media have put there. For example, I have very little real contact with North Philadelphia, the poor section of town. I hear about it and see images of it in the local newspaper. If I relied only on that newspaper for my sense of the place, I'd have a very limited picture to work with. The newspaper, run and owned by Whites, presents what might be called a White picture of North Philadelphia. News stories operate with the presupposition that the reality of a world in which Whites have money and Blacks do not is normal rather than objectionable. That underlying assumption or presupposition is never spoken about and never made visible in news stories, but it limits the range of stories told in the newspaper. Certain stories that do not conform to that presupposition will be routinely and almost unconsciously left out, while those that do conform will be included. A story by a Black that argued for a redistribution of wealth so that everyone had enough cash to get by comfortably, both Black and White, would be out of step with the newspaper's normal "tone." It would appear too "radical" or not sufficiently "mainstream." Yet equally objectionable stories by Whites that portray Blacks as animalistic and violent are considered normal. They conform to the dominant presupposition of the newspaper that Blacks are "normally" and in an acceptable way poor.

For example, a headline on February 15, 2009, consists of these words: "Cold-Blooded Killer." It refers to a Black man who shot and killed a White police officer who was responding to a fight. A sub-headline reads, "The Suspect: Ramsey Calls Career Criminal, 33, 'Unsalvageable.'" In the first paragraph of the story, Police Commissioner Charles Ramsey describes the as-yet-unnamed perpetrator as someone who "should not have been among us, period." The suspect is finally named and humanized in the fourth paragraph, well after the reader has had him depicted as unworthy of sympathy or understanding.[1]

The distribution of information over and across paragraphs arranged in a certain order is called *narrative*. We tell the narrative or story of things, events, people, and the world when we describe it in a certain order. Narratives usually have a subject, the doer of the action or the voice of the story teller. Here the subject is Ramsey, and the object of his story narrative, the story he tells, is the Black suspect. This perfectly normal narrative strategy – of having an authoritative White policeman recount the story of what happened using highly evaluative words such as "career criminal" – has the effect of aligning the reader with the White police and against the Black population. The Blacks are objects and do not get to tell stories about events. Those who do get to tell such stories, the ones who are privileged or dominant, are White.

Surprisingly, perhaps, when one compares the leading "mainstream" US newspaper, the *New York Times*, with comparable newspapers in Britain and Canada, it becomes clear that it is rare for Americans to try to see world conflicts in which the US is involved from the perspective of the adversary. It is much easier for newspapers not involved in conflicts to do this. The *New York Times* features a large collection of articles on the Taliban, Hamas, and other enemy combatants; however, almost without exception, the articles are written with no input from the combatants themselves. Articles about the Taliban generally are "objective" and distanced from the reality of the lives of those who become Taliban and decide to fight the US.[2] In contrast, the Canadian newspaper the *Globe and Mail* featured a section called "Talking to the Taliban," a collection of 42 videos of Taliban fighters responding to a standardized list of questions.[3]

The *Globe and Mail*'s discussions with Afghani villagers make clear that the identity tag *Taliban* covers a range of people, some of whom are not "militants" or "radicals" but are in fact ordinary people who became radicalized by US bombing of their villages. This alternative "narrative" to the one presented by the *New York Times*, in which villagers appear as objects rather than subjects of stories, also makes points of view and perspectives accessible that do not "normally" get represented in the US media. One result of this difference is that Canadians are more reluctant to endorse sending Canadian troops to support the US war effort in Afghanistan.

What this comparison suggests is that the content of news narratives is not determined by the objects and events described alone. The perspective or point of view of the person or institution telling the story makes a difference. Perspective always frames events. A frame is an invisible demarcation that defines the boundaries of a news story, and it differentiates between what will be included and what will be excluded from the story. To get a sense of what this means, imagine being high up in a building overlooking a city. From that perspective, you can see an enormous amount; you can apparently grasp lots of information and data about the city. But you cannot see faces or hear voices; you miss a great deal of detail and information. Now, imagine standing on a street in the city. You can see much less and much more. Your range of vision is limited in a different way by your new perspective or point of view. There is a more visible frame created around your vision (and your potential narrative of what you see) by virtue of the fact that you can only see one part of the street, and the walls of the surrounding buildings prevent you from seeing beyond or around them. But you are now closer to the texture and detail of people's lives; you hear their voices and see their faces. Your news narrative is likely to appear less impersonal. In the example above, the *New York Times* is comparable to the perspective from the top of the building; it aims for a big picture that misses detail and that especially misses the detail of the lives of the Taliban. Instead, they appear as objects, small and in the distance, and as a result, they are easier to depict and to treat as enemies. The particular news strategy coincides with the national interest of promoting the war in Afghanistan in a particular way that harms civilians by bombing villages. The street-level perspective is more akin to what one sees in the *Globe and Mail*. People's faces, if you will, come into focus more readily, and one gets to know them in person as it were. It is harder to treat them as objects who should be killed because they have seen civilian relatives killed by US bombing raids.

If frames both limit and expand what a news narrative can contain in regard to information and texture, the way we see and the tools we use to describe what we see also play a significant role in shaping and determining the content of news narratives. Because we have pictures in our mind with which we compare new data (objects, events, and people) that we encounter, we often pre-interpret the world around us. That makes our operations in it easier. We know, for example, that a man in a suit is likely to be a professional, so we do not have to waste a lot of time trying to figure out what he is, time we would have to spend grasping an entirely new creature covered in green slime with six arms. But those pre-interpretive categories in our mind also lead us to prejudge the world at times. For example, if we learn from our national media to think of Arabs using the category *terrorists* because our news routinely categorizes Arab opponents of US national interests in that way, we are more likely to not allow new information about Arabs to disturb those categories and that picture we have of the world before us. Our interpretations, the categories and images we have in our minds, take precedence to new versions of those categories and images that challenge their veracity and accuracy.

Words express ideas, and words in news stories evoke the ideas or categories with which they are linked in our minds. Words are tools for describing the world, but they are infused with our assumptions, our presuppositions, our framing perspectives, and our interpretations. To append the word *terrorist* to Arabs is not to describe an object or a reality; it is to attach a previous assumption or experience to a new one and to generalize from a particular, limited example (Arabs who did commit terrorist acts) to a group (all Arabs are terrorists). What words are used in the news is very important, then, because words generate images in our minds that tap into presuppositions and interpretations based on past experience that may not always be relevant to new experiences or that may not be applicable to a whole group.

To get a more concrete sense of how frames and interpretations work in news, let's consider the example of the Middle East.

When polled, most Americans side with Israel, but most Europeans side with the Palestinians. Clearly, each group or population has a very different picture in their minds of what is transpiring in the Middle East. How did those differing pictures get painted?

First a few facts. Jews once lived in the Middle East, and were driven away by the Romans. They began to return in the late nineteenth century and eventually controlled about one third of the territory of what was then called Palestine. In 1948 the United Nations partitioned Palestine into two parts, a new state of Israel and a state called Palestine. A civil war followed that Israel won, and many Palestinians were driven out of Israel and have continued to live in refugee camps in adjacent countries. After a war in 1967, Israel occupied all of Palestine. After many years of occupation, it set aside certain areas for the Palestinians to control. It allowed Israelis to establish settlements in Palestine; built new Israeli neighborhoods and towns on Palestinian territory around Jerusalem, a Palestinian city; and exercised violent military repression against any Palestinian who objected to the policy of colonization.

Europeans see the Palestinians as the victims of Israeli colonialism. That is because European news describes the situation differently from the US news media. To get a sense of what form these differences take, it is instructive to compare news accounts of the Israeli invasion of Gaza, a Palestinian-controlled area, in 2008.

The coverage in the *New York Times* portrays the Palestinian defenders against the Israeli invasion as practicing trickery that gets civilians killed. They dress as civilians and hide near schools from which they attack invading Israeli soldiers. These discursive strategies or ways of describing the events make the Israeli invasion appear justified. The Hamas or Palestinian defenders appear to be in the wrong. In one news story, an Israeli attack on a school is excused because it occurred in a "densely packed Jabaliya refugee camp" that is "in a crowded neighborhood full of Hamas fighters." Israeli sources are given priority over others, and the newspaper reports that "mortar fire from the school compound prompted Israeli forces to return fire. The Israeli mortar rounds killed as many as 40 people outside the school."[4] Information about the bombing that might incriminate the

Israeli Army in a war crime is given, but it is qualified by information such as the mention of the Hamas fighters that makes the Israeli bombing seem a defensive action.

In another *New York Times* news account, the Palestinian defenders are more explicitly characterized negatively. They dress in civilian clothes, and they engage in trickery rather than fighting in the open. Gaza, it reports, has been turned into

> a deadly maze of tunnels, booby traps and sophisticated roadside bombs. Weapons are hidden in mosques, schoolyards and civilian houses, and the leadership's war room is a bunker beneath Gaza's largest hospital, Israeli intelligence officials say. Unwilling to take Israel's bait and come into the open, Hamas militants are fighting in civilian clothes; even the police have been ordered to take off their uniforms.[5]

Implicit in this description is the assumption that if the Palestinians use civilian locations such as schoolyards and hospitals to conduct their military efforts, then the Israelis are justified in attacking such sites. Notice that much of the information presented as fact is a report by Israeli intelligence, but one does not learn this fact until the end of a long sentence laying out Israeli intelligence assertions as facts, so that the facts are not presented as being a skewed report by the invaders designed to justify the invasion. Sometimes the placement of a phrase such as "according to Israeli intelligence" can make all the difference. Placed at the beginning of a report, it frames it as opinion, but placed at the end, it is a qualifier to material presented already as fact. The *New York Times* did not take the trouble to talk to Hamas and to find out what their intelligence service was saying about the Israeli invasion.

The reporting by the *Times* was at times even more polemical. In this account, the school attack is explicitly justified:

> Your unit, on the edges of the northern Gaza town of Jabaliya, has taken mortar fire from the crowded refugee camp nearby. You prepare to return fire, and perhaps you notice – or perhaps you don't, even though it's on your map – that there is a United Nations school just there, full of displaced Gazans. You know that international law allows you to protect your soldiers and return fire, but also demands that you ensure that there is no excessive harm to civilians. Do you remember all that in the chaos? You pick GPS-guided mortars, which are supposed to be accurate and of a specific explosive force, and fire back. In the end, you kill some Hamas fighters but also,

the United Nations says, more than 40 civilians, some of them children. Have you committed a war crime? Deciding requires an investigation into battlefield circumstances that cannot be carried out while the fighting rages, and such judgments are especially difficult in urban guerrilla warfare, when fighters like Hamas live among the civilian population and take shelter there. While Israel is the focus of most criticism, legal experts agree that Hamas, a radical Islamic group classified by the United States and Europe as terrorist, violates international law.[6]

The account is a good example of how perspective and point of view work to frame and limit events so that pre-interpretations take precedence to fact. The reporter explicitly adopts the perspective of an Israeli soldier, thus forcing the reader to identify with the Israeli Army and to assume as true their positions regarding the conflict. The Palestinians are portrayed as attackers (when in fact they are the victims of an invasion that is part of an ongoing colonization effort), and careful reminders are dropped in to qualify the actions in favor of the Israelis. The reader is reminded that the Hamas defendants are categorized as a terrorist group and that international law protects the Israeli Army from charges of criminal behavior of they are defending themselves. It is reporting with a distinct edge in favor of Israel.

The reporting of the same event by non-American news sources was quite different. Often, as I noted, events take on different meanings/ simply through the different placement of a phrase or a piece of information. The *New York Times* story of the school bombing privileges the Israeli account. Before even mentioning the number killed, it notes that "Israel said that a preliminary investigation showed that mortar fire from the school compound prompted Israeli forces to return fire."[7] This excuse takes precedence even to the simple reporting of facts, a fairly obvious instance of polemical pre-interpretation. In contrast, the Canadian *Globe and Mail* reports the same events this way:

At least 40 Palestinian civilians were killed by Israeli mortar shells yesterday in a tragedy that could mark the beginning of the end of the current Israel-Hamas fighting in Gaza. The people, residents of the Jabalya refugee camp north of Gaza City, had sought refuge from the advance of Israeli forces in a United Nations school for girls. Those forces, according to Israeli military spokesmen, came under mortar fire, and returned with fire of their own. Israeli tanks and troops blazed into towns across the Gaza Strip yesterday, striking Hamas targets as Arab states pressed for a UN Security Council resolution for an immediate end to combat in the Gaza Strip and deployment of an international force to monitor a ceasefire and protect Palestinian civilians. At the United Nations in New York, Secretary-General Ban Ki-moon called the attack on the school "totally unacceptable" and the UN demanded an investigation. Israeli media, however, played down the event. Its main evening news program opened, not with the Palestinian deaths in Jabalya, but with a story of the four Israeli soldiers killed in the previous 24 hours. All had been felled by errant shots from fellow Israeli forces. The Jabalya school deaths were the third item on the newscast, following a piece on the funeral of one of the soldiers, an Israeli Druze. Commenting on the Jabalya tragedy, an IDF [Israeli Army] spokesman said that troops had fired mortar rounds at the school only after militants barricaded inside shot mortar shells at the Israeli forces. ... The deaths bring the total number of Palestinians killed in 11 days of fighting to 660, Gaza medical staff say. That figure does not include the number of Hamas militants Israel is said to have slain during the three days of its ground assault.[8]

Notice how this report takes into account what is wrong with the *NYT* reporting. It comments on the excuses offered by the Israeli Army for an atrocity rather accepting them at face value. It thus avoids using them to frame and preempt the reporting of the facts of the war crime. It also pointedly juxtaposes excuses with facts, placing the Israeli Army claim that Palestinian resistance fighters were using civilians as human shields with a statistic regarding the huge number of Palestinian civilians killed during the invasion. The implication is that not all of them could have been simple "human shields." And it uses verbs such as *blazed*, which suggest the overwhelming use of force by the Israeli Army against a largely civilian population.

News reporting often merely reports recent facts and fails to contextualize events by providing a sense of history. The *Globe and Mail* avoids this by supplying some historical background to the events in Gaza:

The first is about provenance: Hamas and Hezbollah did not exist before 1982. They are the ideological stepchildren of the Likud party and Ariel Sharon, whose embrace of violence, racism and colonization as the means of dealing with occupied Arab populations ultimately generated a will to resist. The trio carrying on Mr. Sharon's legacy – Ehud Olmert, Ehud Barak and Tzipi Livni – seem blind to the fact that the more force Israel uses, the greater the response in the form of more effective resistance. The second analogy is about technical proficiency. Hamas and Hezbollah have both increased their ability to use assorted rockets to harass Israel. And they are better able to protect their launchers from pre-emptive Israeli attacks. The number of Israeli dead in recent years is in the low hundreds, compared with the thousands of Palestinians killed by Israel. But body counts are not the most useful criteria in this analysis. The real measure is the nagging Israeli sense of vulnerability and the Palestinian sense of empowerment and defiance. It is a gruesome but tangible victory for Hamas simply to be able to keep firing 30 or 40 rockets a day at southern Israel, while Israel destroys much of the security and civilian infrastructure in Gaza. The frustration in Israel is reflected in its bombing attacks on the Islamic University and the Palestinian parliament building in Gaza – symbols of the sort of modernity and democracy that Israel and the U.S. claim they seek to promote in the Arab world. Palestinians and Lebanese pay a high price for their "victories" – but until someone offers a more cost-effective way of dealing with Israel's violence, we will see this cycle of warfare continue for some time.[9]

This report also polemicizes, but it does so in a more historically informed way, and it challenges official excuses rather than reinforces them.

In recent years, the conservative Fox News Channel has acquired a reputation for especially biased reporting of news. It does tell viewers about a selected set of events, but it usually skews the presentation so that conservative assumptions get reinforced. Those would include the following: "the real problem is not already rich executives taking too much wealth out of the economy for themselves; the real problem is immigrants"; "wealthy investors and businessmen are always right; everyone else embodied in their government representatives are always wrong"; and "if we let the wealthy play at making themselves more wealthy in a 'free market,' good will result; if anyone tries to stop them, evil will result." It is instructive to compare a Fox "report" with a regular news report. Here is CNN on the debates regarding President Barack Obama's economic stimulus package in the US Congress. The reporter speaks over an image of President Obama waving to a crowd in Fort Myers, Florida, on the right.

> Yesterday, in Fort Myers, a guy who works at McDonald's was saying how he needed greater benefits. There was a woman recently unemployed who was pleading with the President. Ah, she said she wanted her own kitchen, needed her own bathroom. We saw the President hugging her at some point. And later today, President Obama is going to be traveling to a constr-

construction site. All of this is really meant to take this debate out of Washington, out of the food fight between Democrats and Democrats, and Democrats and Republicans, and simply say: look, this is a situation that involves real people. I get it, therefore push forward this stimulus package.[10]

The report describes a speaking engagement by President Obama in Fort Myers, a community that lost a large number of jobs in the construction trades as a result of the economic recession the stimulus plan was designed to address. Notice how it speaks to the reality that Obama is himself addressing – people in trouble because of the recession. The report stays close to the "facts" that are the real subject of the story.

Now consider Fox on the same day about the same issue – Congress' consideration of the President's economic stimulus bill:

Someone slipped some interesting language into the healthcare system, into that massive bill that will change the way you are taken care of. ... [T]his is a no exit system. You can choose a different insurance company. You can go to a doctor and not have it covered. Under this system, all your medical treatments will be in that database. And furthermore, physicians should be very concerned about the vagueness of this language because it empowers the – the, ah, head of HHS, Health and Human Services, ah, to decide who is a meaningful user of the system and then to impose, quote, "ever stringent measures," increasingly stringent measures to enforce compliance. That's not the kind of vague laws we use in a democracy.[11]

The last remark is a breach of the normal rules of news reporting. It introduces an explicit opinion into the report and breaks down the standard barrier between editorializing and news reporting. But notice as well that the "report" focuses on a hot-button conservative issue – the use of government power to protect people from powerful, usually conservative economic agents such as health insurance companies that routinely deny care to people who need it and ration care to those who can afford to pay large amounts of money for it. The stimulus bill would restrain them and monitor them to make sure they are providing care. Fox, a conservative mouthpiece, would object to such a move by people acting through their government to protect themselves because it levels the playing field in the economic warfare between large private corporations and the larger population.

Student Exercise

You might watch the documentary film *Outfoxed*, which is about the bias in Fox News. Then study a newscast by Fox in comparison to a newscase by one of the less political news organizations such as CBS.

Or, on any given day, buy three or four newspapers and then go online and track down foreign newspapers such as the *Globe and Mail* or the *Guardian*, and compare how they all report on the same event.

Notes

1. "Cold-Blooded Killer," *Philadelphia Inquirer*, February 15, 2009, http://www.philly.com (accessed October 10, 2009).
2. See, for example, "The Taliban's Rising Tide" (editorial), *New York Times*, July 11, 2008, http://www.nytimes.com/2008/07/11/opinion/11fri1.html (accessed October 10, 2009).
3. Graeme Smith, "Talking to the Taliban," *Globe and Mail*, http://www.theglobeandmail.com/talkingtothetaliban/ (accessed October 10, 2009). Extracts from the *Globe and Mail* are copyright CTVglobemedia Publishing Inc. All rights reserved.
4. Taghreed El-Khodary, "Grief and Rage at Stricken Gaza School," *New York Times*, January 7, 2009, http://www.nytimes.com/2009/01/08/world/middleeast/08scene.html (accessed October 10, 2009).
5. Steven Erlanger, "A Gaza War Full of Traps and Trickery," *New York Times*, January 10, 2009, http://www.nytimes.com/2009/01/11/world/middleeast/11hamas.html (accessed October 10, 2009). All rights reserved. Used by permission and protected by the Copyright Laws of the United States. The printing, copying, redistribution, or retransmission of the Material without express written permission is prohibited.
6. Steven Erlanger, "Weighing Crimes and Ethics in the Fog of Urban Warfare," *New York Times*, January 16, 2009, http://www.nytimes.com/2009/01/17/world/middleeast/17israel.html?ref=middleeast (accessed October 10, 2009).
7. Erlanger, "Weighing Crimes and Ethics."
8. "Israel Pounds Gaza by Air," *Globe and Mail*, January 8, 2009, http://v1.theglobeandmail.com/servlet/story/RTGAM.20090105.wvmideast_update0105/VideoStory/specialComment/?pid=RTGAM.20090106.wgaza_main07 (accessed October 10, 2009).
9. "Why It's Hard to Beat Hamas," *Globe and Mail*, January 8, 2009, http://v1.theglobeandmail.com/servlet/story/RTGAM.20090106.wcogaza07/BNStory/International (accessed October 10, 2009).

10. CNN.com, "Transcripts," http://transcripts.cnn.com/TRANSCRIPTS/0902/11/cnr.01.html (accessed October 10, 2009).
11. Fox News, "Breaking News," http://www.foxnews.com (accessed October 10, 2009).

Sources

See Eoin Devereux, ed., *Media Studies: Key Issues and Debates* (Los Angeles, 2007); Paul Marris and Sue Thornham, eds., *Media Studies: A Reader* (New York, 2000); Mark Levy and Michael Gurevitch, eds., *Defining Media Studies* (New York, 1994); Nick Lacey, *Narrative and Genre: Key Concepts in Media Studies* (New York, 2000); Andrew Tolson, *Mediations: Text and Discourse in Media Studies* (New York, 1996); Martin Harrison, *TV News: Whose Bias? A Casebook Analysis of Strikes, Television, and Media* (Edison, NJ, 1985); Paschal Preston, *Making the News: Journalism and News Cultures in Europe* (London, 2009); and Louann Haarman and Linda Lombardo, *Evaluation and Stance in War News: A Linguistic Analysis of American, British, and Italian Television News Reporting of the 2003 Iraqi War* (London, 2009).

11

Visual Culture

with Brett Ingram

Our life – for those of us with the gift of sight at least – is visual. We know the world and live the world visually. The images in our eyes are our most vivid engagement with the world around us, almost more vivid than the words, sounds, and ideas in our minds – the other major contact points between us and our cultural world. Those images come to us from many sources – the news, movies, the Internet, magazines, and so on. Each image is like a peephole in that it only affords us a very limited vision of things that have a much greater amplitude. Most images come to us as part of narratives, stories that pattern our experience of the world in a temporal sequence that is also logical and is informed with valuations. Images of the Taliban in Afghanistan or Pakistan depict them as violent aggressors in a story of warfare with good and bad characters. The logic of the story is moral, and the valuations embedded in it make us experience the events depicted in a certain way. It is as if our everyday experience of the world were not that different from a movie in that we order the visual world by converting the random information that comes to us into stories that explain it and endow the randomness with moral and other kinds of meaning. For the longest time when I was young I "saw" the Soviet Union through the lens of images from popular movies that portrayed communists as dark and threatening, sinister and unkind. It took years of reading and study and contact with actual communists to realize that those images were not entirely accurate. And I learned that those responsible for making them were themselves often guilty of crimes against humanity committed to prevent what communism rep-resented or called for – a fair and equal distribution of wealth – from occurring. But the story that was in my mind when I was young was the one the film media put there, and the visual images that imprinted on my brain became a way of explaining the world I lived in. The visual images I absorbed from American culture explained the visual images I encountered as I lived.

In a similar way, we experience our lives as if we are characters in a story still in the process of being composed, and judge our experiences according to whether or not they conform to certain narrative conventions. We feel confusion and disappointment when someone who has conducted her life honorably suddenly dies, while an individual who we've identified as a "bad" person lives and prospers. This is not how the story is supposed go. Likewise, when we are rewarded for doing the "right" thing, our expectations are met: we got what we deserved. But where do we acquire this sense of what "properly" comes next? The answer to that question determines how we, and society as a whole, make sense of and act in the world. Increasingly, we look not to written texts such as books and poems for the storylines that guide our lives, but rather to *visual culture*. This encompasses television, films, advertisements, photographs, comic books ... anything that relays its story primarily through pictures and images rather than text and words. The study of visual culture proposes that if the world is indeed a stage, as William Shakespeare suggested, and each individual a performer, then when we evaluate the performance, we have to take into consideration not only the script, but also the bodies of the actors, the lighting and set design, the makeup and costumes, the layout of the venue, the appearance of the advertising posters, and the printed pictures that accompany reviews. All of these elements work together to produce meaning, and people interested in visual culture attempt to tease apart how images become saturated with discourses, ideologies, and power.

Many critics argue that the visual has even greater ability to shape people's beliefs than does written text and spoken words. Just think of the folk wisdom surrounding visuality: "A picture is worth a thousand words," "Seeing is believing," and "Out of sight, out of mind." We tend to trust that which we can see as immediate and transparent, whereas words arouse our suspicion as potential tools for deception. However, the inherent faith people have in visuality is the very thing that makes it such an effective way of transmitting ideas meant to construct a sense of reality that favors some and disadvantages others. In order to analyze and critique visual culture, we must attempt to bracket our emotional response to images, to view them with a skeptical eye and ask: why am I being shown these particular images? Who selected them? What would change if I viewed this object or event from another perspective? What story is being told through the things I'm seeing? What behaviors and attitudes are being rewarded, and which are being punished? What different stories could be told, and why are they not?

The cultural supremacy of visual communication is a relatively recent phenomenon. In pre-modern societies, the myths and legends that shaped the social group were passed from generation to generation through oral performances, or recorded in painstakingly handcrafted texts which were only decipherable to an elite minority who had access to the education required for reading literacy. For the vast majority of the population, the reach of a story's influence was limited by the audience's ability to memorize and recite what they had heard. In order to receive and transmit information, a person had to hone his or her faculties for listening comprehension and mental concentration. This style of communication required tremendous cooperative effort on the part of both the sender and receiver of a story. With the widespread use of the printing press in the early eighteenth century, the production of texts and the spread of literacy to the masses increased dramatically, enabling the rise of democracy and consumer capitalism, and heralding the first instances of what would come to be known as mass culture: cheaply produced and widely available books, music, newspapers, and periodicals that connected individuals and communities dispersed by space into a cohesive group united by the shared consumption of common texts. This made possible a much more diversified social experience, as individuals could move from one textual encounter to the next with ease. A reader can "converse" with multiple, conflicting voices as quickly as he can turn the pages of the newspaper or take books off the library shelf. It enlarged the world, insofar as people had increased access to different ideas and perspectives, but also, in another respect, narrowed it: the institutions that owned the technology for producing and distributing texts also controlled the kinds of stories being told. Depending on the degree of openness fostered by the ruling bloc of a particular society, this technology held the potential to greatly expand or severely constrict the range of ideas and information circulating throughout a culture.

In the mid-twentieth century, film, television, and other mass-produced visual media inaugurated a new kind of cultural literacy and mass audience. Traditional oral and literary practices demanded a great deal of intellectual effort from listeners or readers, who had to mentally visualize the events described in words and texts. Visual media, on the other hand, do the work of bringing language to vivid life for us. We no longer have to picture in our minds the events we're listening to or reading about: it's all there on the screen, waiting for us to watch. Some commentators believe that visual media make it "too easy" for the viewer to uncritically accept the meanings given to him by the producers of a visual text. Of particular concern is the almost indisputable fact that visual media has eclipsed all other social institutions – including family, religion, and government – as the preeminent source of the *dominant narratives* that shape social existence. Dominant narratives are the stories we most frequently tell ourselves and each other to give meaning to the past, to make sense of the present, and to predict with some degree of confidence what will happen in the future. They symbolize an imperfect but relatively coherent cultural consensus, and lend a sense of logic and causality to the activities we are compelled to undertake in order to maintain our existence and assume our role in the social order. We must labor to survive in nature, but the capitalist "success myth" – striving for the "American dream" – gives an imaginative purpose to our toils, and lends credence to a certain hierarchical way of structuring work and the distribution of resources. The desire for sexual stimulation and intimacy is common to virtually everyone, but it is the narrative of heterosexual romance and state-sanctioned marriage that guides what is widely held to be a "normal" life trajectory. We are all forced to confront the finitude of our lives, but the story of eternal life after death makes the mortal suffering we endure bearable, even noble. These narratives of work, love, and death don't emerge from a void, untouched by the hands of living men and women and unmarked by human self-interest (although in order to maintain their perpetual viability, such stories must reflexively proclaim their natural, or supernatural, origins). They are constructed by real people in time and both respond to and create the conditions through which a particular version of social organization and human experience takes place.

In visual culture, the values that structure dominant narratives are often circulated through mythical stories that condense the complexities of existence into simplified conflicts between good and evil. In American hero myths, for instance, to return society to a state of equilibrium, the hero simply defeats the villain, who represents the forces which challenge social stability. Of course, there is no single form of "evil" that we as a society are called upon to combat over and over again, but rather, we perceive and target different kinds of antagonistic forces at different times. An iconic American hero may be compelled to take on Nazis in the 1940s, Communists in the 1950s, domestic social oppression in the 1960s, and domestic social permissiveness in the 1970s. And while iconic heroes usually fight for some variation of "truth, justice, and the American way," they are also instrumental in shaping how we come to define those ideas. Heroes aren't by definition conservative or progressive; they are liminal figures who act as proxies for audience members who are themselves working through stressful changes in social reality. For example, when Spiderman was introduced in a 1962 comic book, his transformation from average teen to freakish insect-human hybrid was attributed to a bite from a radioactive spider. This reflected widespread Cold War–era concerns about the existential dangers presented by the proliferation of atomic power. In the 2002 film version of *Spiderman*, the spider is genetically altered rather than radioactive, and the Green Goblin's evil nature results from a scientific research project, funded by the military and undertaken by a giant corporation, that goes horribly awry. These narrative substitutions are indicative of a shift in the focus of public anxiety from the threat of nuclear annihilation to advances in biotechnology which threaten our sense of what it is to be human. Similarly, the *X-Men* comic series, first published in 1963, called the mutant heroes "Children of the Atom," suggesting that their mutation was the by-product of nuclear proliferation. The 2000 *X-Men* movie more vaguely accounts for mutation as a process of accelerated evolution, implying that genetic variation, even of the most extreme sort, is a natural inevitability rather than a human elective. The mutants are metaphors for all groups which are feared and persecuted on the basis of biological traits that make them different from the dominant majority. The film is a sustained attack on conservative policies – represented in the narrative by Senator Kelly's Mutant Registration Act – of intolerance toward sexual and racial Otherness. *X-Men*, in its latest incarnation, deals pointedly with a contemporary social conflict in which greater respect for cultural diversity is opposed by forces dedicated to thwarting progressive change through discipline and surveillance.

However, even as *Spiderman* and *X-Men* make gestures of protest toward some established power structures, such as the military-corporate complex and right-wing authoritarianism, they also reinforce other traditional understandings and expectations of the world. Both films foreground White, heterosexual male protagonists (Peter Parker/Wolverine) who are compelled to reluctantly abandon their normal lives (as a high school student/a cage-fighting loner) in order to rescue a helpless damsel-in-distress (Mary Jane/Rogue) from the clutches of a bad man (the Green Goblin/Magneto) and almost single-handedly save the community (in both cases, New York City). This is a story we've heard and seen many times before. The narrative conventions that underpin both films can be traced back to ancient Greek myths and wind their way through the knight tales of the Middle Ages and the Westerns of John Wayne and Clint Eastwood. They promote an ideology that posits men as leaders and women as passive victims or rewards, celebrates individualism and violence as opposed to community and diplomacy, and locates the source of society's ills in the aberrant behavior of solitary madmen rather than in the systemic problems of exploitative power structures. We can see that America's dominant narratives, disseminated through visual media such as comic books and Hollywood films, are both historically consistent and subject to revision as times change. They draw from the past while pointing toward the future, and are capable of being simultaneously conservative and progressive. They address the desires and anxieties felt by the masses by channeling these emotions through the actions of individual characters in popular stories.

It might seem inevitable that visual media should glorify the perspective of the individual. When we watch a film or a television show, we get the impression of seeing through someone else's eyes. But whose eyes, exactly? Sometimes the answer is obvious, such as when we slowly stalk a swimmer from the shark's point of view in *Jaws*, or watch Agent Clarice Starling fumble in the darkness through the killer's night vision goggles in *Silence of the Lambs*. But in most other cases, it is less clear-cut. We experience a sense of ghostly disembodiment as the camera shows us scenes from vantage points unattainable to a corporeal being. We hover invisibly over characters' shoulders as they converse with one another; we float above great battles, impervious to bullets; we explore from all angles, without fear of being caught, the bodies of couples engaged in the most intimate activities. Because we've become acclimated to the process by which our gaze is woven seamlessly into the visual narrative, our identification with the camera has been rendered virtually unconscious – we rarely stop to ponder why we're seeing things the way we are, we just accept it as a natural part of the viewing experience. To indulge in media spectacles is to temporarily, willingly surrender some element of our control over the world to someone, or something, else; we see what "it" wants us to see, and if the illusion is successful, we feel what it wants us to feel. Much of the pleasure we derive from watching visual media is due to the opportunity they give us to relinquish personal responsibility and slip into a mental state of, if not total passivity, then relaxed participation. We let the camera do the work of moving us about the cinematic world. Among critics interested in exploring the power dynamics of media spectatorship, the nature of our identification with the camera's gaze – particularly in regard to the politics of gender – has been an area rich with theoretical speculation.

Many film critics, inspired by Laura Mulvey's landmark 1970s essay "Visual Pleasure in Narrative Cinema," claim that the classical Hollywood style of filmmaking puts the audience spectator in the masculine subject position, and represents the female characters on screen as objects of desire. They argue that in conventional films, the spatial and temporal distinctions between the gazes of the male director, the camera, the male character, and the spectator are collapsed so that they all seem to be the same thing, and that this unified gaze is directed toward the female character. This makes a heterosexual, masculine way of perceiving the world seem natural and normal because we consistently share his point of view when we consume visual media. The ideological effects of this process extend beyond the theater experience and carry over into everyday life, so that we no longer question the objectification of women or patriarchal dominance in general because we are so accustomed to "seeing things his way." The spectator, male or female, derives pleasure from the experience of voyeuristically viewing women through the eyes, and therefore the sensibilities, of a heterosexual man. Obviously, this not only affects the way men look at and understand women, but also contributes to how women are encouraged to view themselves, that is, as objects to be looked at and desired rather than as active, empowered subjects. Consider how many times you've been pulled along as a camera lovingly, or lecherously, peers at the eroticized details of a woman's body. From *Rear Window* to *Animal House* to *Blue Velvet* to *Basic Instinct*, some of Hollywood's most famous scenes involve the voyeuristic spectatorial thrill of seeing exposed women without being seen in return. Now think of the number of times you've witnessed full-frontal male nudity onscreen, or saw an explicit representation of male sexual arousal. The vast differential between the frequencies of these occurrences suggests a fundamental disparity in gender power not only in visual culture, but also in society as a whole.

The camera is not merely a tool people use to record fragments of reality. It is also a machine that produces ways of seeing which are intentional, persuasive, and invested with power. In our visual culture, media technology intervenes between our eyes and the physical environment to an astonishing degree. Compare, for a moment, that which you know about the world from unmediated bodily experience and that which you know from images captured and reproduced by cameras and computers. We all have an idea of what Earth looks like, but unless you're one of the few humans who have actually floated in space, you are relying on a representation of someone else's vision to form this idea. In the same spirit, most average Americans have never physically traveled to Iran, or Pakistan, or south-central Los Angeles for that matter, and yet they are regularly called upon to make political decisions that have a profound impact upon people who live in these places. The opinions we form and the actions we take are often based upon little else than the limited range of visual representations made available through the mass media. The screen doesn't represent a window that allows us to traverse time and space and gain unfettered access to distant places, any more than taking a tour on a glass-bottomed boat gives us a complete idea of what's happening under the entire ocean. Someone chooses where to point the camera, just as someone decides where to steer the boat, and these judgments determine how we'll perceive and think about what we see.

It may be more productive to think of the screen as a two-way mirror rather than as a window. A window suggests that we, as viewers, are autonomous, fully formed individuals looking out at the world from a position of self-mastery. But what we see on the screens that surround us influences not only how we understand the outside world, but also how we come to understand ourselves. We cannot recognize ourselves as individuals until we see representations of ourselves. With our own eyes, we can only see fragments of our bodies – our hands, feet, the front part of our torsos, a portion of our backs – but there remains significant territory that is by nature off-limits to our unmediated perception, and therefore unknowable, incomplete. We can only know ourselves completely with the aid of an intervening medium – the mirror – which allows us to see ourselves as objects; we become ourselves by objectifying ourselves. But, to take the metaphor further, in a two-way mirror, there is someone else there, watching us watch ourselves. We know we are being watched, but it is unclear by whom. Nevertheless, this knowledge leads us to act in certain ways, to perform in a style that communicates who we are. The screen of visual culture works in similar ways: it gazes at us even as we gaze at it. It simultaneously reflects us and creates us.

Visual culture doesn't operate in a vacuum; it exists in a symbiotic relation to the lives of real people in real places. For example, a media phenomenon such as *Sex and the City* draws upon the desires, anxieties, and values of many women who are trying to reconcile the contradictory paradigms of traditional femininity (associated with motherhood and marriage) and third-wave feminism (characterized by sexual independence and economic self-sufficiency). The show was hailed as groundbreaking because it avoided setting up a simple binary in which women must identify with, and be identified as, either virgins or whores, idealized mothers or erotic temptresses, Madonnas or Mary Magdalenes. Instead, through its main characters it offered a series of gradations along a continuum of socially acceptable models of contemporary femininity. There is Samantha, an ambitious publicist who exhibits the uninhibited sexual voracity usually coded as hyper-masculine; Carrie, a conflicted writer who struggles to bring together her "feminine" need for romantic love with her "masculine" desire for professional success; Miranda, a well-heeled lawyer and unmarried mother negotiating a relationship with a sensitive, working-class man; and Charlotte, a sexually prudish art dealer who unabashedly yearns for a husband to take care of her and a baby she can nurture. The show offered a postmodern twist on the old-fashioned melodrama, a genre that traditionally involves female characters suffering emotional loss as a result of their determination to behave in a virtuous manner. We may not immediately associate the women of *Sex and the City* with the customary meaning of "virtue," but the show is ultimately rather conservative in its definition of what constitutes a life properly lived: three of the four protagonists achieve this by cultivating a monogamous, romantic relationship with a man who is capable of ensuring them a lifestyle marked by conspicuous consumption and respectable class status.

Even as *Sex and the City* challenged some traditional feminine values, such as the prohibition against women seeking sexual pleasure for its own sake, in other ways it worked to maintain gender stereotypes by framing women as vain, materialistic, and emotional. It may be argued that the show simply wouldn't "make sense" if the female characters were primarily motivated by political power, social justice, or intellectual curiosity, but this is the point: what we see on the screen both *reflects* what falls within the realm of possibility in the real world – what "makes sense" – and *creates* that range of acceptable possibilities that constitutes the so-called mainstream by showing us what is "normal." That which is not represented on screen seems undesirable, perverse, or nonsensical when it's encountered in reality because we have all internalized codes that instruct us about how to interpret such dissonant possibilities. Looming over this process is the capitalist market, which is concerned first and foremost with selling goods and services. The expansion of women's sexual freedom may be a notable social advancement, but what is most important to the media conglomerate which produces the show is that viewers are repeatedly exposed to the idea that the solution to human problems can be found in buying and consuming. Sometimes social advancements are good for business; that which is controversial and new tends to attract inquisitive audiences, and tonight's viewers are tomorrow's shoppers. Indeed, the marketing tagline for the *Sex and the City* DVD is a quote from Carrie, directed toward her millionaire love interest, in response to his reluctance to get married: "Don't give me a diamond, give me a bigger closet!" What could potentially be a politically charged, oppositional statement (a mutually agreed-upon rejection of traditional marriage) is reframed as an appeal for even greater consumption (more expensive shoes can heal any emotional wound). Even as one ideal of normality is being challenged, it is replaced by sleight-of-hand with another, no less ideologically invested alternative. *Sex and the City*, like so many superficially subversive mainstream media texts, did not seek to overthrow old value systems for the sake of progressive social change, but rather to shift the balance of cultural power away from social institutions such the church and the family, and toward the private sphere of consumer capitalism.

Visual culture holds a mirror to contemporary life because it both represents elements of a preexisting reality, and constitutes reality-in-the-making by encouraging people to organize their own experience through imitation of what they see on the screen. *Sex and the City*, for instance, implicitly poses the question: which one of these women are you? If we turn our gaze from the television screen to the computer screen, we find that this question is made quite explicit: there are hundreds of online quizzes called "What *Sex and the City* Character Are You?" The quiz confronts the test taker, presumed to be heterosexual and female, with questions about her sexual predilections, emotional tendencies, aesthetic sensibilities, and professional and romantic aspirations, and life philosophies, and then, as its title suggests, reveals which character best represents her. Of course, *none of the above* is not a possible answer or result. The suggestion is that every woman fits into one of these four categories; the show, and the accompanying quiz, "screen out," as it were, the idiosyncrasies and contradictions that make lived experience so confusing, particularly for women poised at the crossroads of conflicting feminist ideals. It offers a way to interpret reality through categorization and differentiation: I am a Charlotte, not a Samantha.

This is not unique to *Sex and the City*, but is a ubiquitous facet of mass-mediated, visual culture. One could just as easily ask, "Which *Real World* Character Are You?" (The Angry Minority? The Promiscuous Girl? The

Alienated Homosexual? The Rowdy Frat Guy?) or "What Alternative Subculture Do You Belong To?" (A Sensitive Emo Girl? A Nerdy Indie Guy? A Streetwise Rapper? A Spacey Hippie?). For every identity, there is an accompanying set of aesthetic, behavioral, and attitudinal expectations that people have internalized through the repetition of their representations in visual culture. It is futile to ask which came first, the social category in reality, or the representation of the social category in visual culture, just as it useless to ask whether your appearance in front of the mirror precedes your reflection on its surface. These relationships are codependent, and integrally connected to one another; in other words, changes in social reality engender changes in media representation, and vice versa. However, this isn't to suggest that we are irrevocably trapped in a world of mediated manipulation. Groups who wish to challenge the way they are perceived in reality may begin by calling attention to ways in which they are unfairly represented in the narratives and images that comprise visual culture.

Visual culture is not only an index of who we are as people. It is also a tangible artistic object, a crafted thing with shape and contour. It always has a spatial and a temporal dimension. The spatial dimension is fabricated through the use of photographic or cinematic techniques such as the placement of a camera or the use of light and set. The temporal dimension is constructed through the assembling of shots or takes into a coherent narrative. Narrative is different from *story*, which is the actual events filmed. Narrative names the string of images that tell that story.

There are other important dimensions of visual culture that enter into storytelling such as characterization and meaning. When a young doctor is asked by a dying girl a third his age to give her one kiss before she dies and does so, the meaning conveyed and depicted is "kindness" rather than something more lurid. Switch the genre or kind of television show it is, and that action might change meaning considerably. Meaning in visual narratives is dependent on context or surroundings, and context can be anything from the genre or kind of visual narrative to the place in the story in which the action occurs. Some things can have multiple meanings, even a kiss, which can be simultaneously an expression of affection and an act of betrayal.

One of the more interesting features of visual culture to examine is the way the same thing is represented differently in different visual situations. Since feminism disturbed the settled order of gender roles beginning in the 1960s, images of women in film especially have given expression to contending attitudes about women's new found independence and power.

In *Fight Club*, for example, Marla Maples, a headstrong and quite independent woman, is portrayed from Jack's perspective as a "ball-buster," while women with cancer who want sex are portrayed as pathetic. No positive women characters appear in the film, and men who are negative or oppressive in some way for Jack, such as Bob, are portrayed as being feminized. Bob is so fat he has breasts. The movie consists in many ways of a move away from emblems of boys oppressed by emblems of mothers (IKEA shopping, womb-like places, breasts, hugs) to assertions of masculine independence from all things associated with femininity and maternal care.

An almost inverse narrative is constructed in *Thelma and Louise*, a film about two women who take a journey away from male power and authority in society and in the family. That power is associated with sexual violation by men. The narrative depicts a move away from oppressive men who would be fathers to women, exercising authority without justification, toward a realm of freedom usually considered to be the purview of men exclusively. That freedom is often associated with the Western film genre, and the women don cowboy attire as they move further toward independence and away from patriarchy. Unlike *Fight Club*, which makes dependent emotional relations seem harmful to a healthy male identity, in this film, relations of mutual support and care are portrayed as positive alternatives to discipline, authority, and violence – all things portrayed positively in *Fight Club*.

Such thematic analysis only gets at a part of how visual culture operates. What is called formal analysis (because it focuses on the form of the image, how it is constructed, rather than what it is about) attends to the way the different techniques for constructing images are used to built narratives, construct characters, make meaning, and tell stories. These formal devices of image, character, and narrative construction often influence what meaning we assign to events and to people in visual narratives.

Consider how a woman who reaches for independence and social authority is depicted visually in *The Silence of the Lambs*. Narrative films of this kind have two formal dimensions. One consists of the way each image is composed; the other consists of how the images are strung together through editing. Clarice Starling is portrayed as a woman who wrestles with emotional limitations (the memory of her dead father) while striving to become a rational FBI investigator. In an early image, she walks into an elevator filled with men taller than she, and the way the image is composed emphasizes her fledgling status within the organization. She in a literal visual sense has a lot of growing to do. But emotions get in the way of her

attaining the rationality she must achieve if she is to become both a successful agent and a successfully de-feminized woman. The film portrays
emotional vulnerability often associated with women (largely perhaps
because men have monopolized public power with all the apparent rationality that goes with it) in a negative light. Clarice must move in the narrative
from a position of vulnerability in which she gets upset easily to one in
which she is able to use her reasoning abilities to capture the criminal. Like
him, a man who is uncertain of his gender identity, she is caught in between
two genders. In one editing sequence, for example, she is depicted getting
upset when a male inmate at an insane asylum flings semen at her; she runs
out of the building and bends over near her car. But an edit occurs, and
the next image we see is her firing a gun at the camera. That dramatic
switch, from an image of vulnerability to an image of competence and
violence, summarizes her entire transformation throughout the film. This
is a film in which a woman becomes a man (if by those terms we mean the
conventional roles assigned each gender in traditional culture).

Student Exercise

Choose a contemporary film or a television show and analyze it
in two dimensions. First, discuss how it links to your particular historical moment. How does it give expression to issues and problems,
fears and desires, and realities and fantasies that are current in your
world? How is the text social, historical, and even political? How
is it about differences in your culture over values, ideals, norms,
and roles? Second, discuss it as a tangible artistic object. How is the
narrative constructed? Does the narrative seem to have a thematic
direction embedded in it? Are images important to the way those
themes are worked out in the narrative? Can you isolate one or two
that strike you as especially important and say why they strike you as
being important?

Sources

See Marquard Smith, *Visual Culture Studies* (London, 2008); Margarita
Dikovitskaya, *Visual Culture: The Study of the Visual after the Cultural Turn*

(Cambridge, Mass., 2005); Richard Howells, *Visual Culture* (Cambridge, UK, 2003); Ron Goulart, *Comic Book Culture: An Illustrated History* (Portland, OR, 2000); Matthew Putz, *Comic Book Culture: Fanboys and True Believers* (Jackson, MS, 1999); and Bradford Wright, *Comic Book Nation: The Transformation of Youth Culture in America* (Baltimore, 2001).

12

Audience, Performance, and Celebrity

Celebrity is both a long-standing feature of human life and a recent invention made possible by communications media that can inspire and maintain ongoing interest, fascination, discussion, and attachment with particular people. Angelina Jolie and Brad Pitt are distinctly modern events, but they also recall a time when an emperor's love affair with an Egyptian queen was the scandal of Rome, something discussed and debated by the city's nobles and commoners alike, a love that was one cause of one of history's most celebrated assassinations. The great religious and political leaders of the past were all celebrities; they possessed a quality that sociologists call *charisma*, a power to inspire trust and attachment in the population as well as to sway minds and influence the course of events. Jesus of Nazareth was such a charismatic celebrity, as was Mohammed of Medina. Alexander the Great was "Great" precisely because he was able to muster a population to form an army to conquer the then-known world. The first universities were organized around celebrity teachers such as Socrates and Aristotle. Before Madonna or Tupac Shakur, Homer sang songs that made him famous, and indeed, his name still lives on as one of the featured celebrities of the literary canon, as much a "must hear" for infatuated Oxford dons as Justin Timberlake is for infatuated teenage girls.

Fame and celebrity status are usually the consequence of one's possessing an extraordinary ability or quality of some kind that sets one apart from others who are not capable of similar achievements or who do not have distinguishing features that make them stand out. Celebrity exalts distinction, the difference of some from others. It separates, divides, and elevates, and it provides a model of distinct greatness that rises above the common lot. Fame in the past was usually associated with recognizably greater talent, be it military, social, cultural, or political. Napoleon Bonaparte was a celebrity because he was a talented military leader who was able to inspire his followers to undertake enormous, difficult ventures in the name of the progressive anti-monarchial ideas he promoted. The Roman writer Ovid was a talented poet who enjoyed notoriety for writing books about how to pick up servant girls in the Coliseum, a rather different version of conquest. Madame de Stael and Mabel Dodge were talented thinkers and cultural leaders who earned celebrity by hosting salons where intellectuals, artists, and bohemians congregated. William Jennings Bryan and Emma Goldman were both celebrity public speakers on political and social issues whose talent earned fame and even notoriety.

Fame and celebrity have evolved and changed with the emergence of new media such as television, magazines, and the Internet. One consequence of the multiplication of media in a capitalist economic context that thrives on the sale of cultural news to consumers in the form of magazines such as *Spin* or television shows such as *Access Hollywood* is that the reasons for celebrity status have become separated from talent. The maintenance of such status has also become more explicitly commercial in motivation. Rudolph Valentino was such a popular celebrity actor in the 1920s that when he died, thousands of women lined up in New York City to view his coffin, but he was a talented actor. Paris Hilton cannot make a similar claim, although her television show, *The Simple Life*, which mocked the idea of the "dumb blonde," entertained with mildly self-mocking irony. Princess Diana's status as a celebrity was less linked to public achievement or to a demonstrable talent in some area of life. She had married a prince and been brave enough to leave him when it was clear there was no love in the match, and that certainly took courage. And her courage further manifested itself in her willingness to engage in physical contact with ostracized people with diseases such as AIDS whose illness provoked fear in others. But such courage followed on her celebrity and was not the occasion for it. It was of a different order from the talent of a singer such as Madonna or an actor such as Kate Winslet. What scholars have noted regarding modern celebrity is that rather than be a matter of achievement or talent or distinction alone, it is accompanied, augmented, and sustained by marketing. In the case of Paris Hilton, marketing seems to have created her celebrity, although blonde good looks might also be considered as much a natural talent as being born with a good singing voice. In the marketing of celebrity, the celebrity is tracked as usual in the celebrity press, but the normal pursuit of information is thought of now in terms of the sale of advertising revenue in magazines or entertainment news shows. The celebrity is on the covers of magazines as much to attract readers as to promote advertised commercial enterprises of various kinds that have only a tangential connection to the celebrity. The purpose of the transaction is not knowledge but profit for the owners of the media in question and the enterprises that advertise in them.

Celebrity may increasingly be a business in a hyper-capitalized world, but, however much "stars" may be produced or manufactured in the contemporary era to sell products or to simply sell news about the individual celebrity, the celebrity cultural system would not work if the audience did not play along by investing interest and emotion in their favorite celebrities. Celebrity is to a large degree democratic; the audience must be seriously interested in the celebrity for that person to be a celebrity in the first place. There must be some reason for the audience's attention, interest, and attachment. That cannot be created by marketing alone, although magazines work diligently to maintain lapsed celebrities such as Jennifer Aniston in public view, stoking interest in people who would pass from view and be forgotten were it not for celebrity marketing.

My experience with celebrity bears out the idea that celebrities are first and foremost matters of personal identity and identification rather than marketing. My first contact with celebrity came in the late 1950s in Ireland. My older brother Don became heavily invested in rock 'n' roll and in the "greaser" look – hair peaked and combed back and laced with oil. Few in our town owned television sets, and our only access to the wider world of entertainment and celebrity was the radio. With the radio came rock music, then becoming increasingly popular. Don identified with Elvis Presley and other similar male singing icons of rock. He kept a photo album into which he put cut-out images of his favorite stars clipped from entertainment magazines. When we came to the United States, this behavior continued, and he continued to dress the part of a young hoodlum modeled on mid-1950s Elvis. What was interesting was that he was a quite sensitive human being with a strong creative and artistic side. In part, the music appealed to that dimension of his personality; such music was creative and open to endless modifications of a simple set of elementary musical, lyrical, and emotional axioms. But he also clearly liked the image of strength the rock greaser look gave him. By identifying with it and by dressing the part, he overcame some of the vulnerability, no doubt, that came with his artistic sensitivity. He looked and could act tough, even if that was not his natural disposition.

There were quite profound temperamental and social reasons for Don's attachment to Elvis, but he would never have even known of Elvis if it were not for the British Broadcasting Corporation, and the BBC would not have known of Elvis unless savvy music industry entrepreneurs had not seen a gold mine in Elvis' talent and marketed it successfully to the world. But they were the medium, not the message. The talent and the aura they saw in Elvis were what attracted Don, and although the pop music magazines enabled him to collect cut-out images of the stars, it was his attachment, his identification with the stars that prompted him to listen to the music and to buy the magazines in the first place, not successful marketing. Why did Don develop such strong attachments to popular celebrities? It gave him companions amongst his male friends who liked similar things and who shared his taste. So it made him feel that he belonged to a community, just as in the past Irish monks might have bonded in monastic communities over their favorite religious celebrities such as Jesus. But did it change his life and provide him with a sense of personal direction, a guide for action in the world, in the way that religious celebrity culture did in the past and still does for many? In a way, yes. "Don't be cruel to a heart that's blue" might be said to be Elvis' first commandment, just as his tenth might be said to be "We can't go on together with suspicious minds; and we can't build our dreams on suspicious minds." This may be the religious moral wisdom of a fallen popular culture imbued with polluted venal commercial interests, but it is comparable to traditional religious instruction in its ability to provide moral direction in everyday life. By now, we all know not to steal (those of us wealthy enough not to have to, at least), but we don't all know not to interact with our loved ones in a suspicious way if we want happiness in life.

Scholars who have interviewed fans of celebrities such as Elvis report that celebrities are more than simply objects of interest. Knowing them is a little like knowing a friend or an intimate, and for many it is probably a way of compensating for the fact that modern life has shed older forms of small town or village or extended family community. People lead more dispersed lives these days than before, and they are more likely as a result to be isolated or to live alone. But even those with full interpersonal lives enjoy celebrity knowledge and celebrity attachment because we all lead imaginary lives along with the ones we lead when we engage with the real world around us. What distinguishes humans from animals is intelligence and imagination, and we use those to create more complex communities than animals are capable of creating. Even when we are not in the presence of those in our personal community of friends or family members, we think of them, we imagine them, and we fantasize about them. Our normal real-world lives are imbued with imagination and fantasy of the kind that one finds in celebrity culture. It should not be surprising then that many people invite celebrities into their imaginary worlds and keep track of them as they might a friend. They also of course take from those imaginary relationships similar emotional gains, feelings of companionship and interest in another's life, and even feelings of concern.

The surfaces and purposes of those imaginary encounters with celebrities are multiple, perhaps as multiple as the types of human personality and the flavors of social ideology. Affect can be quite positive, as in fan adoration of rock stars, but it can also be negative, as when a fan stalks and kills a celebrity like John Lennon with whom he has become obsessed. The range of emotions recalls basic human forms of relating, and celebrity attachment is no doubt built on primary emotional attachments of the kind that characterize human life in general. Those range from over-invested obsession to rage against a hated object that one feels is a threat or a disappointment in regard to one's needs. The ability, even the need, to attach to others seems an essential part of our psychological constitution. We begin attached to another's body, then as we grow we become attached to other family members, then to our friends and lovers. We become human through our attachments; our selfish core becomes social, mediated, civil. Celebrity attachment is thus an iteration or version of something essentially human about all of us. And because human emotional experience is far from singular, fan attachments to celebrities probably differentiate along a fairly broad range.

Some seek the stability and strength that many seek in parents. One way of understanding conservative political movements such as Nazism is to think of them as operating in the same way as celebrity attachments of a quite primitive atavistic kind – a longing for power and control that one lacks in oneself and a channel for negative affect against others who are thought of as responsible for one's sense of powerlessness. Others seek an intimacy and sense of emotional attachment that may be lacking in their lives.

That adolescents are prone to celebrity attachment suggests that that vulnerable stage of life may be a time when those with an unstable self seek external stabilizers. In adolescence, one is uncertain about how one's new self appears in the eyes of others, how one's body fits with the ideal images prevalent in most modern cultures that are highly commercialized, and whether or not one will succeed both interpersonally and professionally in life. Adolescent fans of movie stars report finding a compensatory ideal in their favorite actor. They enjoy imagining themselves in the roles the star actor plays in; it allows them to step outside of their ordinary lives and to take on a more ideal identity, one often associated with good looks and with personal strength that many adolescents feel is wanting in them. Celebrity attachment also takes them out of either troubled or simply ordinary, unremarkable lives and allows them to experience something more extraordinary.

Celebrities are "larger than life" and help to augment those who attach to them. In a sense, celebrities are means of self-empowerment. Celebrity attachment also quite obviously tends toward more positive and equal forms of affect, much like a relationship with a friend or a family member. Fans report feeling that television celebrities are their companions, and when the celebrity is sick, they are missed as a friend is missed. The celebrity, especially those who fill in lonely times of the day such as the morning for those at home, becomes a surrogate friend.

Contemporary life under capitalist auspices consists of work and entertainment. The lives of those on the bottom rungs provide few avenues for the kind of augmented sense of self-importance that comes with having great wealth and social power. Those people will not be successfully creative professionals or entrepreneurs. Not surprisingly, they are especially prone to celebrity attachment. Celebrity culture makes sense in a society in which not everyone gets to be important or fulfilled or recognized. Celebrity identification allows one access to a small, highly mediated version of such things. To identify with a star is to leave oneself and to change place, to become someone else momentarily. It is to leave an old overly familiar world behind and to enter, briefly, a new and quite different one characterized by ample wealth usually and the freedom of movement and of behavior such wealth permits one. But there are a variety of attitudes toward such celebrity freedom. Some feel liberated by it, and some of a more conservative persuasion feel it is worthy of punishment. Women celebrities, especially such as Princess Diana, Paris Hilton, Britney Spears, and Lindsay Lohan, are as much reviled as revered in the celebrity press. And the conservative gossip press, which would favor more traditional identities for women, are especially hard on these female celebrities. Their frequent tumbles from grace into drug or alcohol rehabilitation or into police custody are occasions for the exercise of moral judgment of the kind that seeks pleasure in the punishment of those who depart too easily from the moral order that some conservative audiences uphold in a somewhat authoritarian and unforgiving fashion. Moral rigidity is a way of maintaining a sense of one's own worth and virtue as someone who plays by the rules, accepts the self-restraints that economic inequality imposes on one, and has no tolerance especially for cheaters who seem to feel they can get along without the hard work and rigid self-discipline that are, in this worldview, everyone's inheritance in life. Such moralism restores to one a sense of value and worth that one's allocation to the lower rungs of economic life deprives one of. It is this psychology and this social group that are played to by right-wing celebrity culture in Rupert Murdoch's tabloids such as the *Daily Mail* in Britain and *Daily News* in New York that assess public persona according to how they conform to a rigidly moral worldview, while nevertheless stoking prurience through mildly pornographic imagery. The mix of desire-inspiring visual images of women and anger against them for their independence and inaccessibility is an understandable feature of a culture in which women, faced with an economically unequal world, must choose mates often on the basis of economic success. What this means, however, is that female celebrities are especially prone to angry gossip such as the following from ShowBizSpy: "Britney Spears is worried that her 'comeback' tour will flop. She's finally got a good head on her shoulders, hasn't she?"[1] And this from Murdoch's *Daily News* is more typical of the vituperative gossip women generate in conservative celebrity culture: "Aniston was in Germany promoting her sad little dog movie, *Marley & Me*, with her sad-sack costar Owen Wilson, doing sad things like eating dog biscuits for the shrieking delight of strangely-dressed Europeans. Jen then volunteered to get down on all fours and eat poop if it meant that everyone would love her again, but the German people – always kind, always understanding – put her to sleep instead."[2] Only for parochial American conservatives would Europeans be "strangely dressed" and a woman be unacceptable for being as strong and intelligent as Aniston obviously is. The purpose of celebrity gossip in this instance is to reinforce a narrow worldview based on pre–civil rights prejudices and antique ideological assumptions.

Britney Spears is an example of a female celebrity who was successful because of her talent but whose career as a celebrity has assumed a life of its own apart entirely from that talent. Spears' success was due entirely to her training in a performing arts school and to her willingness to undergo the usual apprenticeship that artists have to undertake. Her 1998 single "Baby One More Time" was a number-one song in America and was followed by other successful recordings such as "Toxic" and by successful tours. But Spears also established herself as a controversial public figure. And her life spun out of control. She married, had children, got divorced, entered drug rehabilitation programs. shaved her head, attacked a paparazzo's car, and became a constant figure on the front cover of grocery store gossip magazines. Nevertheless, by 2009, she had turned her life around, had a successful comeback single in "Womanizer," and won another Album of the Year award with *Blackout*.

Comments on celebrities in magazines, on television, and online constitute a discourse, a particular organization of language and of possible language acts that as much create the object they are describing as record an objective description of it. An objective description of Spears might include physical facts, biographical data, record of accomplishments, and the like. But once one begins to add adjectives, the description cease to be objective and becomes subjective, something inside the viewer instead of the object viewed. For example, a particularly strong adjective would be *slutty* (as opposed to the more neutral *sexy*) because it contains a negative value judgment. Much celebrity gossip discourse contains such value judgments. Examining where such judgments come from and what they mean is as interesting a concern of cultural studies as the celebrities themselves. Indeed, one could say that to be a celebrity is to have meaning for people and that those meanings often appear as discursive acts that project onto the celebrity grids of moral value that make him or her an occasion for exercising moral judgment. Celebrities are a way of testing and reinforcing moral values. But what kinds of values are at issue, and how do they connect with the particular communities that engage in such acts of valuation?

Cultural studies scholars noticed at one point that the discourse regarding Spears shifted from her to her parents and to her mother especially, who was portrayed in the discourse as exploiting her daughter's sexuality and talent to enrich herself. She was also characterized as a failed mother who pushed her daughter out into the world too soon and failed to look after her properly. This discourse was distinctly middle class because it differentiated its own supposedly more wholesome and healthy family values from those of Lynne Spears, in part because she was depicted as White trash, a reference to poor or working-class rural, often Southern, people (Lynne Spears is from Louisiana). According to the ideal paradigm of this middle-class discourse, women should be decorous, deferential, and selfless rather than ambitious, independent, and forceful in the pursuit of career goals. Motherhood in the discourse is moralized; Spears' mother was blamed for her daughter's dysfunctional behavior. Because she supposedly failed as a parent, her daughter spun out of control. In a move typical of this moral discourse, Lynne Spears was portrayed as having over-indulged her daughter instead of having set firm boundaries for her. The discipline that capitalism requires of those on the bottom rungs is thus internalized by those who inhabit those rungs and turned into a sign of virtue. Others are judged by how well they align themselves with the ideal of self-discipline and self-control, an ideal that identifies the requisite personal identity of individualist capitalism with white middle-class values.

Consider this example of gossip that appeared shortly after Spears made her comeback:

> Gotta hand it to Papa Spears. He's managed to find the right drug cocktail (with a little professional help, of course). He makes sure she's wearing underwear when she goes out. He makes her wash her hair more than once a week, and he keeps the Luftis and Adnans away. He can't keep them all away, though. With the release of *Circus*, all the parasites who fed on Britney's fame and fortune have come out of the woodwork to feast anew. Chief leech and former husband Kevin Federline has even "opened up" to *People* magazine. K-Fed still doesn't have a job, but he's more than happy to talk for hours about life with Britney, life after Britney, and the two little people who made it all possible: Sean and Jayden. He manages to portray himself as a good father, but that's not surprising considering all the hired help he has. $20,000 a month buys a lot of nanny.
>
> Also oozing her way out of obscurity is her loser "cousin" Alli, who scored an interview with *In Touch Weekly* to bitch about how she was banished from Britney's life. Well, yeah. She was getting paid to be an assistant, not an enabler. She now claims to be concerned about Britney's welfare, saying, "How can they say Britney is sick and then shove her out on the road, with all that pressure?" Hey, honey, somebody's gotta pay all those people.[3]

Notice how laced with value judgments this excerpt is, judgments that mix morality in with even everyday events such as washing hair (bad not to), wearing underwear (bad not to), taking drugs (bad to do so, at least those of which this moral value system disapproves – alcohol not included), and so on. Notice too that parents are portrayed negatively if they have any other motive than that sanctioned by the discourse. This moral sensibility is often associated with personal toughness (I can put up with hard knocks; why can't you?), and it is interesting that this hard-bitten cynicism of the economy's lower rungs appears as a caustic comment on a more liberal-sounding expression of care regarding Spears and her illness. Those who get away with things in this discourse, especially those who earn money without a hard life and hard effort, are judged negatively. It is as much a social position speaking as a person.

Student Exercise

Pick a celebrity you are interested in or are interested in studying, and look up the gossip that is written about him or her on such sites as prettyboring.com or ShowBizSpy.com. Analyze a gossip segment for the values it contains.

Notes

1. "Britney Spears Worried Tour Will Flop," ShowBizSpy.com, March 2, 2009, http://www.showbizspy.com/article/182617/britney-spears-worried-tour-will-flop.html (accessed October 10, 2009).
2. "Jennifer Aniston, Owen Wilson Plug 'Marley & Me' with Doggie Feast," *New York Daily News*, March 2, 2009, http://www.nydailynews.com/gossip/2009/03/02/2009-03-02_jennifer_aniston_owen_wilson_plug_marley.html (accessed October 10, 2009).
3. Lisa Vogle Songer, "Britney Spears, Comeback Queen," Pretty Boring, http://www.prettyboring.com/?q=node/9344 (accessed October 10, 2009).

Sources

On Celebrity Culture, see Paul McCaffrey, ed., *Celebrity Culture in the United States* (New York, 2008); Sean Redmond and Su Holmes, eds., *Stardom and Celebrity: A Reader* (Los Angeles, 2007); Su Holmes and Sean Redmond, *Framing Celebrity: New Directions in Celebrity Culture* (London, 2006); P. David Marshall, *The Celebrity Culture Reader* (New York, 2006); Ellis Cashmore, *Celebrity/Culture* (Abingdon, UK, 2006); Chris Rojek, *Celebrity* (London, 2001); and P. David Marshall, *Celebrity and Power: Fame in Contemporary Culture* (Minneapolis, Minn., 1997). On Britney Spears, see Leah Greenblatt, "Britney Gets Back in the Ring: A Report from Her New Tour," *Entertainment Weekly*, no. 1040 (March 27, 2009): 13; "Britney Spears," Gossip Center, http://www.celebrity-gossip.net/celebrities/category/C5 (accessed October 10, 2009); and "Britney Spears," CelebritySpider.com, http://www.celebrityspider.com/britneyspears.html (accessed October 10, 2009).

13

Bodies and Things

Culture also happens in bodies and to bodies. Body culture takes the form of how we walk and talk, how we bear or carry ourselves, and what "image" we project. If the way we style our physical selves depends on our thoughts or concerns about how others see us, then one could say that the culture of bodies is in part social, and it depends on mental imagery – the thoughts in our minds regarding how others perceive us – that plays an important role in shaping our physicality. To the degree that imagery is cultural or human-made, our physical existence is cultured and cultural. What we take in from others through our minds shapes our physical selves. But concomitantly, we project mental images into others' minds through our bodily actions. Our bodies engage in cultural action on our behalf. Some young men think of themselves as gangsters, and they hold themselves in certain postures as a result, and they walk in a distinct manner, one that projects threat and the possibility of violence. Certain women bend their bodies to the ideal images of perfect good looks that circulate in the culture around them. Their way of carrying themselves seeks to project attractiveness, instead of toughness and strength. One task of cultural analysis is to explain these differences.

As part of our cultural experience, we inhabit bodies and interact with things in the world around us in meaningful ways. How we move our bodies through space expresses our identity, our sense of who we are, and that sense of physical identity often is influenced by our sense of how others see us. Who we are to a degree depends on how we are perceived by others around us. Such perceptions can change our own perceptions and feelings about ourselves. A white male businessman in a suit can afford to walk briskly and with a sense of confidence. He sees himself as possessing financial power, and his way of dressing and behaving attracts a gaze from others that confirms his impression of himself. An ethnic minority woman, especially one with dark skin, in the United States will in all likelihood feel less confirmed in her identity by her surroundings, especially in the world of business; fewer women of color inhabit the higher echelons of financial success for one thing. As a result, she will in all likelihood dress and move differently, and the attention she attracts will also be different.

Our bodily demeanor can thus be an index of how the world makes us feel about ourselves – whether we walk upright and proudly or bent over and stooped, for example, and whether we look up and ahead or down and away. And those feelings can register real attitudes that affect people's lives in substantial ways. Studies have shown that tall women get better jobs than shorter women. And women students of color in the sciences have a more difficult time establishing themselves as credible participants in the performance of expertise in their academic scientific communities. They have to work to achieve the same level of assurance in their voices that come more easily and readily to their fellow white male and female students. If they have large bodies – larger than normal breasts, for example – they are treated and looked at differently. As a result, large-bodied women of color in the sciences feel they have to work harder to achieve the respect and acceptance that comes almost automatically to their equally smart white, especially male, colleagues.

Physical cultural studies are concerned with bodily life – everything from body shape and its significance to dance and the different meanings it has in different cultural contexts. Bodies change meaning depending on the context in which they are found. A strappingly muscular body in men used to be a sign of moral health and heterosexual masculinity, but in recent years, it has come often to signify gay male identity, since many young gay men celebrate physical beauty and cultivate it. And even within the muscle-building community, different bodies have different meanings. The hyper-developed body of some champion builders appears strange and even ugly to outsiders, but for those within the community who know the codes and recognize the signs of achievement, the "over"-built body is a token of success, a sign of hard work.

The cultural significance of bodies resides not only in what they mean but also in how they are inhabited, used, and experienced. One's experience of one's body can be affected by one's cultural surroundings and by the media. The meaning they have for us can change as a result. Consider the female breast. It has a biological function in that it is used to feed infants. But it is assigned a sexual or erotic meaning in certain cultures that it is not assigned in others. When Janet Jackson allowed a breast to be exposed on a nationally televised event, it provoked a scandal in the United States. But in parts of Africa, women live with exposed breasts and do not use clothing such as brassieres to cover and to support them. No scandals ensue because the cultural meaning of an exposed breast is different in Africa. In some parts of Africa, upright, hemispherical breasts are considered attractive, while other social groups favor long pendulous breasts. But the exposure of the body part lacks moral significance. However, the spread of media globally, with much of it coming from the developed countries of the West and travelling East and South through the countries of Africa, has meant that the West's cultural codes regarding sexuality have also spread. In the Western media, women's breasts are highly eroticized and considered an important feature of female sexual attractiveness. As a result, women in Africa have had to change their assumptions about their own bodies. In the past, the removal of a breast as a consequence of breast cancer would not have occasioned concern regarding sexual attractiveness. But as one African woman put it, once it was discovered by African women that "the breast was a sexual organ," mastectomies became more vexed as medical procedures because they were seen as negatively affecting sexual attractiveness.

Girls are especially prone to influence regarding body shape and weight. Gina is a 24-year-old woman from Colombia who came to America when she was 18. She talks about how her physical sense of herself changed when she emigrated. In Colombia, she was considered too skinny, so none of the boys paid any attention to her. Men there, she says, prefer women with big bottoms and large breasts. So for them, Gina, who is slender and has what is called a "boy's body" shaped like an hourglass – narrow at the waist and long legged – was not seen as attractive. When she came to America, her sense of her physical self changed. Suddenly, she was in a culture where her build was considered very attractive. She became sexually active as a result and ceased being the shy young woman she had been up to that point. Now, when she goes back to Colombia, things are different. Her face has changed to reflect her new sense of confidence and her greater sexual experience. She carries herself differently and walks somewhat jauntily.

Gina's bodily experience is not unique. Women in Western-influenced cultures live immersed in images and stories that express cultural expectations regarding women's bodies. Cultural ideals of "beauty" get identified with certain shapes and sizes, often to the psychological and emotional detriment of those whose bodies do not conform to the standard. And increasingly men are subject to similar influences concerning everything from bodily hair to weight. But the role of culture in our physical and material lives is far more pervasive than the codes and conventions of appearance and attractiveness. The medical care of the body is cultural as well, and when the swine flu erupted in Mexico in the spring of 2009, culture played a role in making the attack more deadly than it had to be. Nearly a hundred people – many more women than men – died because the culture of sickness and medicine in Mexico, especially amongst the poor, is such that people go to doctors only when illness becomes very grave. Up to that point, they prefer to medicate themselves using folk medicines that are sold without prescription. As a result of beliefs that people absorb from the culture around them, many more people sought treatment for the flu too late for it to be effective. And many more died as a result than had to.

Culture affects the treatment of severe illness even when one enters the professional medical community; it is not only poor people who allow cultural attitudes to affect how they behave. When doctors in America treat patients with severe illness, the culture of health care in the US, which is private and profit driven, means that doctors must train patients with severe trauma from car accidents or gunshots (themselves, of course, culturally influenced events) much more quickly than doctors in social welfare countries in Europe such as Denmark. In those countries, government-sponsored healthcare means that patients are allowed to spend much longer in treatment. American doctors must encourage patients to be self-sufficient sooner so that they can survive on their own outside the for-profit system that tries to minimize the amount of time they spend in expensive hospitals. As a result, when conducting swallowing therapy, for example, with patients who need to relearn elementary bodily activities after traumatic injuries, American doctors use spoken instructions and do not touch or assist the patients with their hands (which might prolong dependency and delay independence). European doctors, in contrast, are more likely to use their hands to assist the patient, since it does not matter how long the patient takes to learn to survive alone. The government sponsored health care system does not need to make sure only the minimum is spent to rehabilitate the patient and does not need to instill independence as quickly so that patients can survive on their own outside the hospital. The US culture of healthcare is different because conservatives were more successful in the US at preventing government-funded healthcare from coming into existence. Such healthcare would have prevented conservatives in business from profiting, through the sale of expensive health insurance, from other people's needs. The more liberal and socialist European culture of healthcare assures that people's needs are met by pooling the resources of the community through taxes for government-funded care.

We also live in constant interaction with the world of things around us. Our lives are sustained by everything from toaster ovens to cars. Contact with things places us in certain kinds of social relations and give us access to certain forms of cultural meaning. When I come into contact with buses, a rare experience for me, I encounter people I would not normally encounter – most recently, a Hispanic mother of several children who worked at a casino and who was headed for the overnight shift just as I was making my way home from work through a snowstorm that made driving a car impossible. I never touch poker chips but if I did inhabit a cultural world in which such objects were common, I would find myself in a completely different social milieu from the one I usually frequent as well as a completely different culture. Instead of a quiet library, I would be in a loud casino. The first time I went to the local Native American bingo hall, I was struck by how gray everyone seemed, and it wasn't just hair. Their skin seemed sallow, as if they came a cultural world in which physical exercise was not common and eating well was not a priority.

Things can be distillates of meaning for communities that bind the people of the community together. A crucifix or a Star of David or a crescent, for example, is a material object with intense significance for particular religious and ethnic communities. All bind different people together in a common shared understanding of the world. Common everyday objects can also have more personal meanings. Marcel Proust in his novel *Remembrance of Things Past* reports that he once tasted a sweet cake called a madeleine and was suddenly reminded of his childhood because he used to eat the same sweet cake when he was young. A whole world of lost recollections was summoned forth by the simple taste of the madeleine. When I was growing up in Ireland, I attended Catholic mass regularly at a time in the 1950s when it was said in Latin and accompanied by incense. Now, whenever I smell incense burning, I am reminded of that church in that small Irish town. A whole world of lost experiences and realities, from the sight of men lying dead in beds seen through windows on narrow streets to the men in fishing boats rowing out to sea to cast nets, is revived by the smell. It has meaning, and it evokes a now gone culture.

Ordinary useful objects also take on meaning from the ambient culture. In certain subsistence level tribal communities in South America, the making of tools is an occupation that requires the effort of the whole tribe at particular times in the year. The objects assist the survival of the community so their manufacture is invested with great meaning. It is far from the ordinary everyday event it appears to be to an outsider for whom the whittling of wood may not be that significant an activity. In the more developed parts of the world, cars have long had both a practical and a symbolic meaning for many people. In recent years, hybrid cars came to signify "cool" and a sense of connection with environmental concerns because the cars use less gas and are less polluting. In the 1960s, on the other hand, the Pontiac GTO was cool to us high school boys, precisely because it had a large V-8 engine that burned enormous amounts of gas in order to go faster. And fast was cooler than environmental awareness back then.

Buildings and monuments are things in our world that are often invested with meaning. The Vatican, for example, is a building with great meaning for many people, even though it is unremarkable from an architectural point of view and is even built incorrectly. For many years, the Brooklyn Bridge was quite meaningful in the lives of New Yorkers because it was the first such bridge in America. A poem was even composed about it. Since 9/11, itself a meaningful thing or event in the lives of many people, the twin towers of the World Trade Center have become significant in ways they were not before, and indeed, it is their significance as icons of US foreign policy arrogance and economic power in the eyes of Islamic radicals that led to their being the target of a terrorist attack.

In your everyday lives, objects or things are charged with meaning you may take for granted. "Hoodies" once were associated with athletes (at least when I was growing up), but now they signify a particular kind of hip subcultural allegiance. Gold jewelry in Black youth culture also has meaning that it lacks in, say, comparable White youth cultures, which might be more consumed with other kinds of accessories such Abercrombie and Fitch clothing. "Hotrod" cars mean more to kids who grow up in "country" culture, where NASCAR is a leading form of entertainment, than they do to urban kids who might find more meaning in tattoos or body jewelry. Similar meanings attach to such lifestyle consumables as vacations and houses, toys and clothes, drugs and computers. Mac or Windows? We're all familiar by now with the cultural difference lodged in these two things, a difference between the hip, artistic, and cool-looking Mac products and the mass market Windows with all of its unhip glitches. To a certain extent, we are what we own. Things define or express our cultural identities as much as words or actions.

We are also what we eat, of course. When we eat food, we literally take in things from the world and make them part of ourselves. What those things are constitutes a culinary lifestyle that is laden with cultural meaning. Cuisines are often specific to particular ethnic or geographic cultures – soul food or Italian pizza, for example. Some foods are significant of a culture of educated healthy eating or of a high level of awareness of the varied cultures of the world, while some reflect economic status more negatively – cheap fast food that is easy to come by but dangerous to one's health.

The study of material culture in Cultural Studies is concerned with the meaning of objects in our lives. Some objects are closely connected to our bodily lives and to our internal emotional lives. For example, the sarong is a colorful garment worn by both men and women in Indonesia that has numerous functions. It is clothing; it communicates social messages; it operates emotionally; it is a token of exchange in rituals such as marriage; it swaddles children and covers corpses. The colors and designs can have religious meaning, but the sarong textiles themselves can also act as "super skins" in that they are extensions of bodily and emotional life. Someone in distress will cover his or her head with a sarong to prevent intrusive communication and to signal a desire to left alone. Sarongs also serve as tokens of social exchange. A particular kind of sarong given as a marriage gift will imply the need for one kind of reciprocal gift over another. Particular sarong designs belong to particular villages, but they can be given away in marriage, as when a bride brings designs with her and weaves them into the life and sarong styles of her new family home. Sarongs are adjusted and worn differently in different social situations. They are worn to the ankles for formal events, and to the knees for work or informal interactions. The way a sarong is worn affects the bodily life of the wearers; a long woman's sarong obliges her to walk in clipped short steps, while a man's looser sarong allows him to take longer strides (much as tight women's skirts force women to walk differently from men). Sarongs are also work garments in that they are used to absorb the liquids of everyday life, everything from menstrual blood to a child's urine. They serve as extensions of the body. A person's sarong is so associated with that person that it accompanies him or her to the grave and is used to wrap the corpse.

Something as simple light is also an important material thing in our lives that has cultural meaning. Light is associated with clarity, truthfulness, trustworthiness, and good knowledge, while darkness or the lack of light often has the cultural meaning of evil or danger. Light alters our sense of space and has a psychological effect on us. It penetrates our being in both positive and negative ways. Light makes spaces seem larger, and its presence can be reassuring. But it can also be used to the point of excess and harm, as when the German government interred radical opponents of capitalism in rooms in which the light was intense and never turned off. The effect was to disorient them and to drive them to suicide. Absence of light, on the other hand, need not always signal danger. It can also be conducive to a sense of safety, comfort, and hominess. In Jordan, in the Bedouin community, tents are dark, but that darkness is associated with safety. Guests are invited into the dark in order to protect them from dangers that might lie outside.

Another interesting "thing" in our cultural lives is kitsch. If you don't know what kitsch is, think "knock-offs" and cheap imitations, such as furniture with gilt that seems expensive but is in fact cheap. Kitsch consists of things that embody an aspiration to have the goods of the wealthy without having the wealth. So kitschy products such as gilt-edged furniture made cheaply allow those with champagne tastes and Budweiser budgets to have what they cannot really have. A sign of kitsch in furniture would be detailed molding work that lacks the kind of fine detail that genuine handcrafted work possesses. Instead, this furniture is usually turned by machines that are incapable of that level of refinement of detail. It looked cheap and clumsy to anyone familiar with "the real thing," but not to those who merely wanted the appearance of the real thing.

How should we interpret something like kitsch? Sociologists associate it with social groups that have less income and less education. Cultural scholars see kitsch as a way for such people to deal with modern life, which uproots old systems of belief and replaces them with commercialism. In traditional culture, religious messages and cultural wisdom are passed on through routine daily communication and rituals, but in modern commercial culture, such cultural processes and institutions are less central; more central are commerce and the advertising messages that turn everyone into potential consumers. Kitsch responds to this situation by using it to gain a traditional sense of the world; we buy cheap things that have exalted value and that provide us with a sense of routine security. They have cohesive meaning and lend us a sense of trust and reassurance. Kitsch provides "cosmic coherence in an unstable world." Kitsch is repetitive rather than creative and unique. It provides a sense of familiarity because it is so routine.

I grew up in a family in Ireland that was poor and that possessed kitsch objects, mostly religious paraphernalia such as statues of the mother of Jesus. My mother listened routinely to *Mrs. Dale's Diary* on the BBC radio channel, a kitschy show that was all about daily routine events and that was kitschy because it imitated more serious drama. It invested everyday life issues with meaning for my mother. And the statues probably had a similar function; here was a statue of a woman who was looked up to and revered – a very different reality from that of my mother, who was trying to raise four children alone on very little income. The statues probably had a healing function, a way of making routine existence seem valuable. Indeed, the very kitschy quality of the objects – that they were not originals but were imitations that were likely similar to those owned by a much larger group of people – in all likelihood was the key to their value: they afforded a sense of community, of belonging to a group that all possessed the same things. They were a way of curing loneliness.

Student Exercise

Choose an example from either physical culture or material culture and interpret it. For physical culture, you might consider weightlifting or cosmetic surgery. For material culture, you might consider something like a particular kind of toy, some common object in home decoration such as figurines, or a popular cultural object such as the artwork on private buses in cities like Calcutta.

Another possibility would be derelict buildings or houses – what do they signify? How do they preserve evidence of past cultures that no longer exist? What do they tell us about social and cultural change?

Sources

See Helen Sheumaker and Shirley Teresa Wajda, eds., *Material Culture in America: Understanding Everyday Life* (Santa Barbara, Calif., 2008); Ian Woodward, *Understanding Material Culture* (London, 2007); Karl Cappett, *Thinking Through Material Culture* (Philadelphia, 2005); Jennifer Hargreaves and Patricia Vertinsky, *Physical Culture, Power, and the Body* (London, 2007); Shari Dworkin, *Body Panic: Gender, Health, and the Selling of Fitness* (New York, 2009); Philip Hancock, ed., *The Body, Culture, and Society* (Buckingham, 2000); Samantha Holland, *Alternative Femininities: Body, Age, and Identity* (New York, 2004); and Sam Binkley, "Kitsch as a Repetitive System," *Journal of Material Culture* 5, no. 2 (2000): 131–152.

14

Transnationality, Globalization, and Postcoloniality

with Hanna Musiol

Culture is often national in character. The culture of Japan is distinct in many respects from that of nearby China. The cultural traditions are different; the current political culture is different. If one moves a little further away, to Indonesia, say, or to India, the differences multiply – according to religion, food tastes, language, literary and musical traditions, and so on. But one would also find similarities between these very different national locations. The same shows might be on television, imports often from one country to the next, or the same Western-style clothing might be on sale in stores. On the radio, one might hear the same international pop music. In many places, culture is both national and transnational, a matter of local production or tradition and a matter of "flow" between nations.

Cultural nationalists endorse the belief that states are politically sovereign entities with clearly defined borders, a unified political and economic system that affects all similarly, and a set of legal and cultural practices shared by its citizens. Nation-states, in such a view, are imagined as more or less homogeneous, culturally and ethnically: culture is produced internally, within a country's borders with little outside influence, and shared by the country's citizens equally. Accordingly, nationalists ignore or reject the transnational dimension of cultures, and, no less importantly the diversity of cultures within one country. Think, for example, how a culture of Native Americans on the Pine Ridge Reservation in South Dakota might differ from that of the financial elite in New York or of Chinese immigrants in San Francisco.

Considered as a transnational phenomenon, culture transcends, undermines, and displaces national borders. In the second half of the twentieth century, the cultures of the former Eastern Bloc in Europe (Czechoslovakia, Hungary, Poland, Romania, and, to a lesser degree, Yugoslavia, Bulgaria, and East Germany) shared many characteristics and traits across national borders, from the structure of their creative industries, to the popularity of the aesthetic movement of social realism, to various forms of national cultural rituals such as military parades. In other words, despite each country's emphasis on its unique ethnic and cultural character, national language, and even open animosity to one another, they shared many cultural traits with their neighbors, all thanks to a participation in a social-ist economic system and a shared experience of existing under Soviet military, political, and economic control. Something similar occurs when national cultures are influenced by the spread globally of American tastes and cultural proclivities, from McDonalds to hip hop, from Facebook to blue jeans, to the extent finally that such things cease to be "American."

Cultures, therefore, are affected by, but not limited to, national bounda-ries. Some cultures are regional in character – the Amazon Basin, for example, or the Pacific Islands, while whole regions such as "Latin" America share cultural assumptions and practices across borders while nevertheless differing remarkably in other ways (from salsa to mariachi in music, for example). A transnational approach to the study of culture is particularly important in the study of stateless and migrant cultures and ethnic groups that are not protected by national or international laws: the Palestinians and the Kurds in the Middle East; the Jews or Roma in Europe; Native Americans; indigenous populations in post-colonial nations in South America, Africa, and Asia; tribal communities in Africa; sexual minorities in most countries; and so on. In some sense, we must speak of a *planetari-ness* of cultures.

Transnationality and globalization and post-coloniality are intercon-nected phenomena and processes. In popular discourse, economic, tech-nological, or military globalization are often presented as the very condition of progress – a one-way process of democratization and modernization of non-European and non–North American states and peoples that starts at the center of Western capitalist democracies and travels worldwide reach-ing all developing countries. It is true that globalization in its many forms connects diverse cultures, economies, and peoples, but the recent collapse of financial markets worldwide; the deregulation of labor laws in countries as diverse as the US, Mexico, and Indonesia; and the environmental deg-radation caused by the unchecked, exploitative policies of transnational companies all reveal the inequality and dangers inherent in such a global connectivity network when it is guided by the immoral principles centered on unrestrained self-interest.

Globalization means a world of "constant motion." But, the movement of capital, migrants, goods, or information is not inherently free-flowing, libratory, or progressive, as neoliberal (pro–free market) ideology would have it. It operates within particular power structures and frameworks. National and international laws, the anti-piracy or copyright laws, for example, regulate the transfer of cultural products such as films, music, computer games, and so on. The flow of goods is subject to international tariff and agreements, such as the North American Free Trade Agreement (NAFTA). The developments of communication and social networking technologies, such as the radio and TV in the beginning of the twentieth century, and the mobile technologies and the Internet (with its Skypes, Facebooks, and Twitters), have accelerated communication over large distances, across national and physical borders, Yet, it would be wrong to idealize the power of such technologies. Although represented in popular culture as easily available and transformative, their depiction in the film *Enemy of the State* (1998) may be just as accurate. Countries like China and Iran routinely seek to filter the Internet and monitor Internet practices for suspicious activities inimical to the state. Google and Yahoo infamously entered the Chinese market under the condition that they ban access to all human rights–related sites or redirect the Internet traffic to pages favoring the views of the government.

One of the most important arguments in cultural studies is that most of the global frameworks that regulate the flow of capital, goods, technology, and information (the World Trade Organization, NAFTA, the World Bank, and so on) have roots in colonial history.

Colonialism refers to the domination of a nation, peoples, or society by another nation through political, military, and economic interventions; territorial expansion/occupation; and various strategies of cultural oppression and coercion (via language, cultural practices, control of media, knowledge, etc.). Colonization was usually based on claims of cultural, racial, technological, or economic inferiority on the part of the colonized peoples, and justified by the dominant power within the rhetoric of development, as a modernizing and civilizing mission. In practice, the colonial systems were ones of economic exploitation and cultural oppression. It is important to note here that the *post* in postcolonial implies the enduring effects of colonial domination, rather than the end of colonialism. For example, although the end of World War II marked a new period for colonized peoples of Africa and Asia, many of the newly established nations in these two continents and in Latin America remained within the sphere of political, economic, military, and cultural influence of the former colonial powers.

If one of the main aspects of colonialism and globalization is that they attempt to impose a uniform ideology of progress, development, and civilization, then one of the most important aspects of cultural studies is to engage with alternative, postcolonial "ways of knowing." For example, at the beginning of the twentieth century, the writings, music, and visual art produced by African Americans in the US were not recognized for their contribution to national culture. Their so-called race books were not taught at schools and universities and were not widely accepted for their value in the study of society until later in the second part of the twentieth century.

The postcolonial approach in cultural studies acknowledges the power of such cultural exclusion and its lingering effects on cultures worldwide. To colonize is to deprive of land and resources, but also to control the representation of that experience. For example, most popular films about France after World War II did not engage with France's colonial history. In 1966, Senegalese filmmaker Ousemane Sembene released *Black Girl* (*La Noire de...*) as an attempt to correct this blindness. Shot in black and white, in the minimalist style of the French New Wave, the film told the story of a French family through the eyes of their Senegalese maid, Diouana. Diouana is excited to leave Senegal and its poverty to pursue a better life in France. Employed to be a nanny by the French middle-class couple, she finds herself to be working as their housemaid. However, she soon learns that her job requires her not only to clean and cook for the white couple. She is also hired to "perform Africa" for them. In the course of the film, the flat on the French Riviera where the French couple reside with their maid becomes a space where the colonial power structure is reenacted daily. Diouana, along with the couples' collection of African masks, is just another trophy of their neocolonial conquest. In the end, unable to come to terms with her new imprisonment, she commits suicide.

In the film, Sembene used a dual-narrative structure. Throughout, the viewers listen to two conflicting narrations: the couple's discussions of Africa and colonialism that always ignore and silence Diouana, and Diouana's internal monologue. By stifling the voices of postcolonial people, and especially of postcolonial women, Sembene argues, the French were able to retain most of their colonial control. Instead, Sembene allowed Diouana's voice to truly take over, and frame the story of one average French family in the context of postcolonial struggle. His film gave voice to a different subjectivity, but also offered a different way of telling stories in cinema.

Transnational cultural studies is also concerned with the way media form and content flow across national borders and between national cultures. In reaction to the experience of colonization, many national cultures have been for some time nationalistic in their cultural policies; they have, like Senegal, tried to maintain a high level of indigenous content in media programming, especially television. This was done by regulating the media and limiting foreign content and foreign private company access to the indigenous cultural market. But with globalization has come an increased penetration of such national enclaves by new media such as satellite television that bring with it content that is distinctly "modern" and that is quite different from the local national culture or cultural experience. As a result, the culture of "modernity" (which is largely American in origin and emphasizes American values and concerns, from the liberal ideal of individual personhood to the popular cultural focus on entertainment as opposed to education) has spread around the world wherever economic development attracts and permits media such as satellite television to exist. Many people around the globe, as a result, share, despite national, regional, and provincial cultural differences, the same sense of what a "modern" lifestyle is or what appropriately "modern" fashions in clothing are. Lady Gaga plays in New York and Lugansk. Television shows about dating and marriage are almost universal, as are reality shows modeled on the British and American originals. A common world experience, juxtaposed to local cultural differences, has emerged. The "look" of cities in China is increasingly the same as that of cities in the West, as entire old cities are razed to make way for buildings considered to be more modern. To young people especially, local historic cultures can appear quaint and even touristic when judged against the new, more modern version of culture that can be seen and heard on international television or radio. Kyoto is a cultural center in Japan where one can see scads of temples, icons of traditional Japanese culture. But you see few young people wandering amongst the temples; they can be found in Tokyo instead, sporting all the latest in modern dress that they have refashioned according to their own creative instincts and listening to modern pop music.

In the past, the influence of one culture on another, especially if it was based on a difference in levels of economic development, was characterized as cultural imperialism or cultural colonization. But increasingly, cultural scholars emphasize the more positive dimension of transnational cultural movements and flows. Traditional cultures can be progressively modified by the dissemination of stories and images of more modern forms of life and of lifestyle (especially regarding such rituals and institutions as mating and marriage that in their more traditional forms were often disadvantageous to women). Young people in Taiwan report that they are attracted to the more modern images of romantic life that they see when they watch imported Japanese television shows. Similarly, teenage girls in the Upper Nile villages of Egypt listen attentively and regularly to the radio that broadcasts melodramas about urban live and urban romance especially. Limited by traditional cultural assumptions about women's lives in their local communities, the radio brings them a vision of freedom from traditional strictures that they aspire to emulate. One of the more interesting developments to observe over the coming years will be the conflict between traditional authoritarian cultures such as China and the modern anti-authoritarian ideas that cultural flows will bring to the country. The question of whether international corporations such as Google and Microsoft will cooperate with the attempt by authoritarians to maintain cultural control will be a significant issue in this regard.

India is a good example of the diverse issues that arise in studying culture in a transnational context. India is a postcolonial country that for centuries was under British rule. About 5 percent of the population speaks English, and the national sport of choice is a British import – cricket. The British created a nation out of many diverse ethnic, cultural, regional, and linguistic parts, and that diversity persists today. Elements of quite traditional culture – such as the practice of arranged marriages or the social divisions along caste lines – exist side by side with elements of modern life such as consumerism, television, and a telecommunications-based lifestyle. India is also a good example of how changes in government regulatory policy can affect a culture. Up until the late 1980s, Indian culture was highly regulated. No foreign corporations were permitted to own the broadcast media; all were state run. And foreign films were limited and little watched. One consequence of this cultural insularity was that the governments elected on the national level tended to be conservative and traditionalist; they sought to preserve the traditional culture that was a core feature of broadcast television, which broadcast *The Ramayana*, one of the religious texts of Hinduism. And that cultural traditionalism no doubt made the success of the conservative politicians more likely at the polls.

But the deregulation of the media meant that private companies could broadcast media content, and anyone could start a cable television network (sometimes with as few as 200 subscribers) if they wanted. The result was that the content of Indian film and television changed; more foreign shows and more foreign films made their way into the market. In the late 1980s, few people went to see American films; now the newly built cineplexes are busy and popular. American and other shows (and their adapted Indian versions) are popular on television. Perhaps as a result, India recently rejected the Hindu traditionalists at the polls and elected a government more committed to economic and cultural modernization.

India's entanglement with globalization has also had profound effects at least on the segment of the population in direct contact with foreign economic penetration in the form of outsourced services such as call centers where Indians answer the telephone and deal with customers in places such as the United States. Such call center workers often have to adopt Western names (Alan instead of Ashok), and they often also have to pretend to be Western. As a result, some report that they come to identify with their new Western self and have difficulty adjusting back, after a long shift at work, to their actual lives and actual identities. Men report that they complain when they get home after a night pretending to be Western about how "Indians" in their own household behave. Often, the complaint is that they are too Indian. This cultural shift toward a desire to emulate a global vision of modernity takes the form of changes in attitude fostered by advertising and the new consumer culture that has taken hold in the global middle class especially. Whereas in the 1980s, the ideal of female beauty in the media was a voluptuous body and while women then scorned western dress (miniskirts and jeans) in favor of traditional saris, since 1991 (the rough start date of the modern media era in India), the ideal of female beauty in the media has become markedly thinner, and fashionable women now wear miniskirts and jeans. In Indian culture, the old contrast between a modestly dressed and therefore virtuous woman and an overly Westernized anti-heroine has disappeared. Middle-class Indians now also report feeling superior to "locals" who cannot afford Western consumer goods and must make do with indigenous products.

The clash between old and new, tradition and modernity, often plays out in the narratives of popular Indian films (referred to as *Bollywood* because they are made in what used to be called *Bombay*, today the city of Mumbai). The arrival of foreign corporations has helped create a new middle class that is associated with the adoption of Western attitudes toward consumption and the more flexible lifestyle (especially in regard to marriage) that one finds in the West, where arranged marriages are a thing of the past and what Indians call "love marriages" are more the norm. Most young people of this social group voice a preference for love marriages, and many films deal with the problems they face as they confront parents committed more to the traditional model. One very popular recent film, *Dilwale Dulhania Le Jayenge* (*Those with the Heart Win the Bride*; 1995), concerns a young couple whose love is stymied by a father who has arranged for his daughter to marry someone from their region in India. But one feature of Indian life is what is called *diaspora*, the dispersion of a sizable population over the globe and especially, in this case, in the United Kingdom. The girl, Simran, makes a trip to Europe, where she meets Raj (the son of a successful Non-Resident Indian businessman from London), and they fall in love. Their courtship features transgressive elements that are common to Bollywood films: faced with a choice at an inn of sleeping in the one available bed together or sleeping in the barn, Simran chooses the barn. Raj lovingly keeps her company, and when she awakes in the morning, he has transferred her to the bed and changed her into pajamas – all done chastely, of course. But he teases her by pretending they made passionate love. As the story unfolds, Simran's father refuses to allow her to escape from the planned marriage, and Raj attempts to insinuate himself into her father's good graces – but to no avail. In a conservative gesture in keeping with the cultural idea of self-sacrifice for women, Simran decides to accept her father's decision. But in the end, when all seems lost, the father finally relents and Simran and Raj are united. The narrative combines elements of tradition and modernity, affirming both the ideal of obedience to fathers and the need to modify the old ways in keeping with more modern practices.

Cross-cultural influence and pollination also lead to the development of cultural hybrids, graftings of the new and the modern onto the local and the indigenous. For example, a popular American show, *The Newlywed Game*, was adapted to India and produced as *Adarsha Dampathigalu* (*The Ideal Couple*). Many shows that are cloned in India are infused with local elements to make them appear less foreign. But some shows are simply global in character and are not easily localized. *Adarsha Dampathigalu*, for example, is about a taboo subject in conservative Hindu society – marital relations and sexuality. In the cultural tradition, women did not often marry across castes, and most marriages were arranged. The dominant cultural myths portray women's anger as more destructive than that of men, and women were trained in the culture to pursue a path from their birth home to the home of their husband. There was no leeway for a "career." Restrictions on women are still prevalent in India, and many programs continue to portray women primarily in traditional service-oriented roles. But the new imported shows that are cloned offer alternative identity possibilities for women. In *Adarsha Dampathigalu*, women are given equal say with their husbands in a way that poses an implicit challenge to the ideology of the Hindu conservative cultural tradition. Nevertheless, the introduction of this foreign hybrid into India required a slow process of acculturation. Initially, the questions asked of contestant couples were general and concerned impersonal issues. But as the show progressed over the years after its introduction in 1994, the questions became more intimate. But as the questions became more intimate, women felt more liberated to put forth ideas that went against India's conservative cultural norms by, for example, suggesting that "love marriages" were as successful and stable as traditional arranged marriages. The moderator of the show always controlled such remarks and reaffirmed the norms that were being challenged. The moderator put his arm around one husband, for example, and said, "You have a good wife. She stepped on the stage with her right foot first, she has brought harmony in your relations with your parents when things were not so good, and she has borne you a child. You are a very lucky man." In this instance, a global and potentially threatening cultural product was made safe for domestic consumption in a way that diminished the threat it posed.

Transnational cultural pollination works in the other direction as well. Cultures that are not dominated by enormous long-standing film industries, for example, that have well-established generic formulas and conventions often can afford to be more inventive than the dominant (especially American) film industry. They also need to be more inventive both stylistically and in terms of thematic range in order to attract attention and to compete with the very popular American films. That inventiveness has caught the eye of American filmmakers such as Quentin Tarantino, who regularly draws on Hong Kong gangster films, for example, in his own movies. And popular Hong Kong films such as *Infernal Affairs* have been remade as American films with an American cast (*The Departed*). It is interesting to compare such remakes to see how cultures differ. One remarkable difference is the emphasis on male-male friendship in Hong Kong movies. Such friendship is less available as a cultural model in America, and in *The Departed*, the emphasis shifts to a more competitive relation between the two primary male characters.

Student Exercise

View *Chungking Express* (1994), a film that makes a motif of transnational cultural influence. What role does the popular American song "California Dreaming" play in the film? How are the characters' lives shaped by globalization? How are the tensions between traditional culture and the new global culture portrayed?

Pick two films from the list below and compare their representations of trans- or intranational travel and migration. What are the conditions of voluntary or involuntary migrations, their causes and effects, according the films? How do the films listed below narrate local and global migrations?

Fighter (2000)
Hotel Rwanda (2004)
Broken Rainbow (1985)
Five Easy Pieces (1970)
Inch'Allah Sunday (*Inch'Allah Dimanche*; 2001)
Head-On (*Gegen die Wand*; 2004)
Perfect Stranger (*Gadjo Dilo*; 1997)

Given the multicultural makeup of Western nations, creative industries in England, Australia, and the US have begun to represent that cultural diversity in films. Pick one pair of films from the list below and think about how they represent multiculturalism and the challenges it poses.

Crash (2004) and *When the Levees Broke* (2006)
Love Actually (2003) and *Dirty Pretty Things* (2002)
Australia (2008) and *Rabbit-Proof Fence* (2002)

Sources

See Divya McMillin, *International Media Studies* (Malden, Mass., 2007); Patrick Murphy and Marwan Kraidy, *Global Media Studies: Ethnographic Perspectives* (New York, 2003); James Curran and Myung-Jin Park, *De-Westernizing Media Studies* (London, 2000); and Diana Crane, Nobuko Kawashima, and Ken-ichi Kawasaki, eds., *Global Culture: Media, Arts, Policy, and Globalization* (New York, 2002).

Index